Special Ways with Ordinary Days

★ ★ ★

by Sharon Meisenheimer

Fearon Teacher Aids
a division of
David S. Lake Publishers
Belmont, California

Illustrations by Marilynn Barr

Entire contents copyright © by Davis S. Lake Publishers,
19 Davis Drive, Belmont, California 94002.

However, the individual purchaser may reproduce designated
materials in this book for classroom and individual use, but
the purchase of this book does not entitle reproduction of
any part for an entire school, district, or system. Such
use is strictly prohibited.

ISBN 0-8224-6347-4

Printed in the United States of America
1. 9 8 7 6 5 4 3 2 1

CONTENTS

Introduction v
Apple Days 1
Balloon Days 7
Box Days 13
Clown Days 19
Cookie Days 25
Dot Days 31
Dragon Days 37
Elephant Days 43
Foot Days 49
Frog Days 55
Giant Days 61
Hat Days 67
Mitten Days 73
Monster Days 79
Mud Days 85
Noise Days 91
Penguin Days 97
Pocket Days 103
Scarecrow Days 109
Squirrel Days 115
String Days 121
Teeny-Tiny Days 127
Umbrella Days 133

INTRODUCTION

Make any ordinary school day a special day for your students with *Special Ways with Ordinary Days*. This book is a collection of one day mini-units that use thematic books, films, poems, and songs as springboards for activities that develop thinking, reading, writing, and motor skills.

Special Ways with Ordinary Days focuses on twenty-three different themes, including apples, dragons, feet, string, and umbrellas. For each theme, there is an open-ended reproducible pattern page, a list of readily available resources, ideas for "bring-from-home" objects, and three Special Day mini-units.

Each Special Day mini-unit includes five parts: Feature Focus, Learning Labs, Think and Talk Time, Project Pursuits, and Movement Models. These parts work together to form a complete thematic one-day unit. Since there is more than one Special Day for each theme, you may "pick and choose" the unit that is best suited for your class.

Feature Focus tells you the books, poems, films, songs, or short stories that are the focal point for each Special Day unit. These resources serve as the springboards for the rest of the activities on the page. Some of the stories and poems mentioned are common fairy tales and nursery rhymes. If you don't have the version mentioned in the Ready Resource list, you may substitute any version of these you wish.

Learning Labs provide suggestions for learning-center activities, matching games, and cooking projects. These ideas are designed for individual or small group investigation and discovery, and will provide children with an excellent opportunity to develop language, motor control, sensory awareness, and basic readiness skills.

Think and Talk Time includes total group activities designed to expand the children's understanding of the theme for the day. These discussion periods will help stimulate the children's imaginations, listening and communication skills, and appreciation for literature and music.

Project Pursuits outline ideas for creative and open-ended projects that reinforce the theme. Many of the Project Pursuit suggestions expand on ideas expressed in the Think and Talk Time section. You can make these art projects and readiness games more simple or more elaborate depending on your students' abilities.

Movement Models contain creative movement activities and structured games for the class or small groups. These activities encourage development of large muscle coordination, strength and balance, and social play.

Suggestions for Incorporating Special Day Themes in Your Classroom

The following is a list of general ideas and activities to help you incorporate a special theme in your classroom and in the curriculum.

1. Set out a selection of books and stories from the Ready Resource list each time you use a Special Day unit. Encourage students to look through and read the books during the day.
2. Use theme items to decorate the classroom. For example, on an Apple Day, pin construction-paper apples, pictures of apple trees, and red and green crepe paper around the room.
3. Adapt simple songs, poems, and games to include the item of the day. For example, you could change the words to the song "London Bridge Is Falling Down," to "Bright green dragons all around."
4. Arrange for field trips and classroom visitors around the different themes—visit the amphibian section of an aquarium during a Frog Day, have a milliner come to class during a Hat Day, take a field trip to a bakery on a Cookie Day.
5. Many of the activities incorporate reading, writing, math, science and social studies skills. You might want to use isolated activites that are appropriate for the subjects you are teaching.

6. Extend a Special Day into a Special Week. Hang a large lettered sign that reads "It is _____ week" on a wall or bulletin board. Incorporate several Special Day activities into your lesson plan each day of the week.
7. Incorporate photographs of the children into the lessons. Use a good camera to take a black and white close-up of each child's face. Duplicate the pictures on a high quality copy machine. Make several copies of each picture for the children to use in projects throughout the year.
8. Involve parents and community by asking them to donate some of the following items:
   * Used clothing—hats, shoes, mittens, jewelry, socks, and shirts.
   * Craft scraps—yarn, felt, upholstery fabrics, thread spools, ribbons, trims, and sequins.
   * Kitchen "throwaways"—milk cartons, soda caps, Styrofoam meat trays, grocery sacks, small jars, egg cartons, margarine tubs, coffee cans, and paper towel rolls.
   * Miscellaneous items—fake flowers, seed and merchandise catalogs, greeting cards, toothbrushes, boxes, wood scraps, wallpaper samples, old menus, and Styrofoam packing pieces.
9. Encourage children to make suggestions for Special Day activities or projects.

Apple Days

Pattern Page

Apple Days

Timing
   Early Fall
   Johnny Appleseed's Birthday (9/26)

What Children Bring
   An apple or an apple product.

Previous Day Reminder
   A construction paper apple pinned to each child's shirt.

Ready Resources

Books
   Aliki. *The Story of Johnny Appleseed.* Englewood Cliffs, NJ: Prentice-Hall, 1963. (See related activities, page 6.)
   Bruna, Dick. *The Apple.* Los Angeles: Price, Stern, Sloan, 1984.
   Gibbons, Gail. *The Seasons of Arnold's Apple Tree.* San Diego, CA: Harcourt Brace Jovanovich, 1984. (See related activities, page 5.)
   Greenaway, Kate. *A-Apple Pie.* New York: Warner, 1886.
   Le Sieg, Theodore. *Ten Apples Up on Top.* New York: Random House, 1961. (See related activities, page 4.)
   McMillan, Bruce. *Apples: How They Grow.* Boston: Houghton Mifflin, 1979. (See related activities, page 5.)
   Nobel, Trinka H. *Apple Tree Christmas.* New York: Dial Books, 1984.
   Rothman, Joel. *A Moment in Time.* Merrick, NY: Scroll Press, 1973.
   Watson, Clyde. *Applebet.* New York: Farrar, Straus & Giroux, 1982.
   _____. *Tom Fox and the Apple Pie.* New York: Crowell, 1960.

Films
   International Film Bureau. *A Visit to Apple Cider Country.* Evanston, IL: Journal Films, 1977. (See related activities, page 5.)

Poems
   Adoff, Arnold. "An Apple." In *Eats: Poems.* New York: Lothrop Books, 1979.
   Cromwell, Liz and Dixie Hibner. "If I Were an Apple." In *Finger Frolics: Fingerplays for Young Children,* rev. ed. Livonia, MI: Partner Press, 1983.
   Scott, Louise B. "Five Juicy Apples." In *Rhymes for Learning Times.* Minneapolis, MN: Denison, 1984.

Short Stories
   O'Brien, Edna. "Magic Apples." In *Tales for the Telling.* Jonathan Lanman, ed. New York: Macmillan, 1986.

Apple Day #1

Feature Focus   Read the book *Ten Apples Up on Top.*

Learning Labs

★ Cut a piece of tagboard into ten long strips. On each strip, draw a picture of apples stacked on top of each other to represent a numeral, 1-10. Laminate and leave in a learning area for the students to sequence.

★ Slice each child's apple into four or five slices. Let the children practice stacking the slices before eating.

Think and Talk Time

★ Retell the story using a flannel board. Cut the characters and apples out of felt and back with sandpaper. Have the students count out the apples as you place them on top of the characters' heads.

★ Discuss the possibility of actually carrying apples on top of one's head. What things *could* be stacked and carried in this manner? Have the children experiment with different things in the room.

★ Use paper apples to create "Up on Top" math problems. For example, place three apples on a table and say, "Here are three apples up on top." Then place two more apples above these and say, "Here are two more apples up on top." Ask the children to tell you how many apples there are all together.

Project Pursuits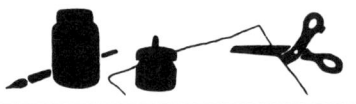

★ Make an "Apples Up on Top" counting book. Have each child contribute a page. Paste a photo of each child's face on a piece of drawing paper. Have the students draw in bodies and backgrounds. Then have each child draw his or her favorite number of apples "up on top" of the photo. Prewrite the following caption on each page: "(name) has (number) apples up on top."

★ Make paper-bag apples. Have each child stuff a paper bag with crumpled newspapers. Twist the tops of the bags and fasten with rubber bands to make the stems. Have the students paint the apples with red, yellow, or green tempera.

Movement Models

★ Play "Apples Up on Top." Have the children try to walk around with pieces of flat foam balanced on their heads. Once they have mastered one piece of foam, add a second piece. See how many pieces of foam each child can carry "up on top."

★ Have the children play "Apple-Balance Relay." Use the paper-bag apples from *Project Pursuits*. (Pick the ones that balance best.) Divide the class into teams and mark off a starting line and a turn-around line. Each child must walk from the starting line to the turn-around line and back again with an apple balanced on his or her head.

Apple Day #2

Feature Focus Visit an apple orchard or a fruit stand, or watch the film *A Visit to Apple Cider Country*. Read the book *Apples: How They Grow* or *The Seasons of Arnold's Apple Tree*.

Learning Labs

★ Create an apple stand in a role-playing area. Supply the children with a basket of plastic apples, plastic or paper bags, and a sign that reads "Apples for Sale."

★ Cut apples and trees out of construction paper. Write numerals on trees. Ask students to put correct number of apples on each tree.

Think and Talk Time

★ Before going on the field trip or watching the film, ask the children to share what they already know about apples and apple trees. Ask questions such as, "Has anyone ever picked apples?" and "How do you think an apple tree changes from season to season?" You may want to broaden the discussion to include other kinds of fruit trees.

★ While on the field trip or while watching the film, ask children to observe the trees and the apples hanging from them. Also ask children to observe the orchard workers.

★ Discuss the seasons and growth cycle of an apple. What kind of weather is needed? How does the tree produce fruit? Why are there bees at or near an orchard? Read one of the books to the children.

Project Pursuits

★ Take pictures at the orchard or have students draw pictures of things they observed in the film. Have the class use the pictures in a class book. Ask students to sequence the pictures and to dictate captions that tell the story of a trip to an orchard.

★ Make individual apple-shaped books for the class. For each child, cut two apples out of red construction paper. Staple drawing paper inside the apple shapes and trim to size. Have the children illustrate and write or dictate a story about apples. You might ask them to write a story about a trip to an orchard, what an apple tree looks like during each season, or how to make apple pie.

★ Provide the children with red, green, white, and brown paint. Ask the children to paint a picture of an apple tree during each of the four seasons.

Movement Models

★ Sing and act out "All Around the Apple Tree." (tune of "Mulberry Bush")
    Here we go round the apple tree,
    the apple tree, the apple tree.
    Here we go round the apple tree,
    on a frosty morning.
Other verses:
    This is the way we climb the ladder . . .
    This is the way we pick the apples . . .
    This is the way we wash the apples . . .
    This is the way we peel the apples . . .
    This is the way we cook the apples . . .
    This is the way we eat the apples . . .
(After the last verse, let the children eat their apples from home.)

★ Play "Apples in Baskets." Provide baskets or boxes for the children to throw balls into. Call the balls "apples." Let the class keep score on a chalkboard, tallying two points for every apple they get into the basket.

Apple Day #3

Feature Focus Read the book *The Story of Johnny Appleseed*.

Learning Labs

★ Cook applesauce with the class. Peel the apples with a mechanical peeler. (Save the peels and the seeds!) Then cut them into pieces. Put the apples in an electric skillet with some water. Cover and cook until tender. Mix in cinnamon and sugar to taste. Let cook one minute longer. Then mash the mixture together until it is smooth enough to eat. Serve in small paper cups.

★ Help students cut yarn the length of each peel. Let them measure the yarn "peels" using standard units of length or using invented units such as arm length, paper-clip chain length, or desk-width length.

Think and Talk Time

★ Read and discuss the story. How did Johnny Appleseed get his name? Why was he important? Why did he do the things he did? What did Johnny learn from his travels?

★ Discuss the applesauce the children made. What was it's texture? How did it taste? Ask the children to think of other foods that are made from apples. Help them see that apples are an important food.

Project Pursuits

★ Make a classroom bulletin board. Place a picture of Johnny Appleseed under an apple tree on a bulletin board. Have each student make a paper apple and place it on the tree. You might have children write their favorite apple products on the apples. Place the caption "Thank You Johnny Appleseed" on the board above the display.

★ Choose a scene from the book for children to illustrate. Supply the children with crayons and drawing paper.

★ Make apple seed designs with the children. Give each child several apple seeds. Have each child arrange and glue the seeds in a design on a piece of tagboard. Ask the children to add to the design using crayons or markers. Display the final work in the classroom.

Movement Models

★ Dramatize one scene from the story. Read the story aloud and pick children to act out the parts of Johnny, and any other people, animals, apples, and seeds in the scene. Change players until everyone has had a chance to participate.

★ Play a game called "Apple Apple, Apple Seed!" Ask the children to stand in a circle. Choose one child to go around the circle and tap each child while saying, "apple apple." When the child taps someone and says, "apple seed," the person that was tapped chases the first child trying to tag him or her before he or she reaches the empty spot in the circle.

★ Play a variation of "Hot Potato" called "Hot Apple." Have the children sit in two circles. Let the children in each circle pass an apple around by tossing it as you play music. When the music stops, whoever is holding the apple is "out." Have the two children who are "out" switch places.

Balloon Days

Pattern Page

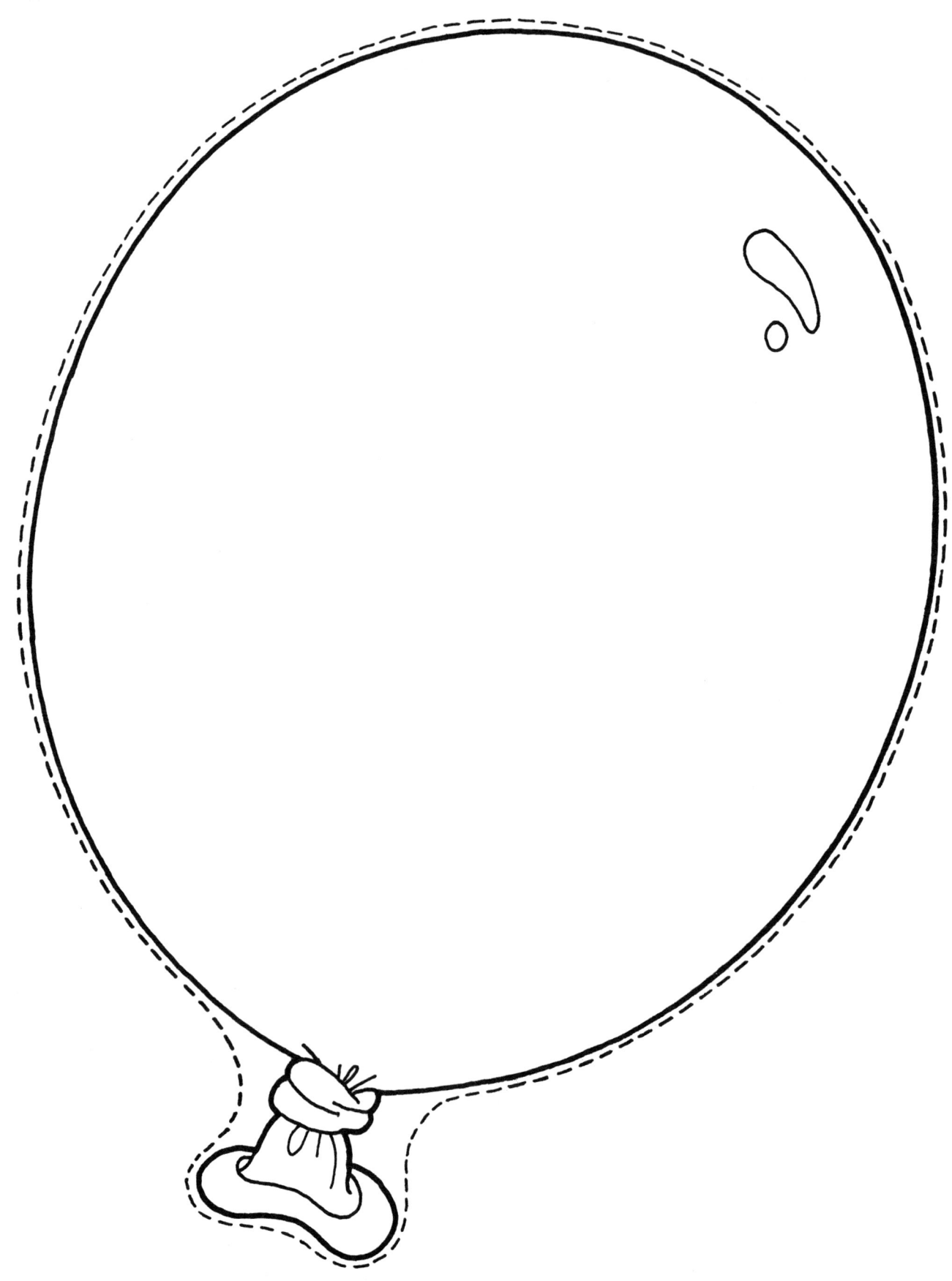

Balloon Days

Timing
>Spring
>During an alphabet unit

Previous Day Preview
>Just before children leave the classroom at the end of the day, have a basket of blown-up balloons brought in. Answer any questions with, "You'll find out tomorrow."

Ready Resources

Books
>Adams, Adrienne. *The Great Valentine's Day Balloon Race.* New York: Scribner, 1980.
>Calhoun, Mary. *Hot-Air Henry.* New York: Morrow, 1981. (See related activities, page 12.)
>Chase, Catherine. *My Balloon.* New York: Dandelion Press, 1979.
>Coerr, Eleanor. *The Big Balloon Race.* New York: Harper & Row, 1981.
>Dean, Anabel. *Up, Up and Away! The Story of Ballooning.* Philadelphia: Westminster Press, 1980.
>Fenton, Edward. *Big Yellow Balloon.* New York: Doubleday, 1967.
>Lamorisse, Albert. *The Red Balloon.* New York: Doubleday, 1978. (See related activities, page 11.)
>Mari, Iela. *The Little Red Balloon.* Woodbury, NY: Barron, 1979.
>Matthias, Catherine. *Too Many Balloons.* Chicago: Childrens Press, 1982.
>McKee, David. *King Rollo and the Balloons.* Mankato, MN: Creative Education, 1982.
>Willard, Nancy. *The Well-Mannered Balloon.* San Diego, CA: Harcourt Brace Jovanovich, 1976.

Films
>*The Balloon Tree.* Santa Monica, CA: Pyramid Films & Video, 1970.
>BBC. *Balloons.* Paramus, NJ: Time-Life Films & Video, 1974.
>Lamorisse, Albert w/Films Montsaceris. *The Red Balloon.* Chicago: Macmillan Films, 1956. (See related activities, page 11.)
>*Magic Balloons.* Deerfield, IL: Learning Corporation of America, 1968.

Poems
>Scott, Louise B. "Balloon Man on the Corner." In *Rhymes for Learning Times.* Minneapolis, MN: Denison, 1984.
>Silverstein, Shel. "Eight Balloons." In *A Light in the Attic.* New York: Harper & Row, 1981. (See related activities, page 10.)

Records and Songs
>The Fifth Dimension. "Up, Up & Away." On *Greatest Hits on Earth.* Arista Records. AL6-8335.

Balloon Day #1

Feature Focus Read the poem "Eight Balloons".

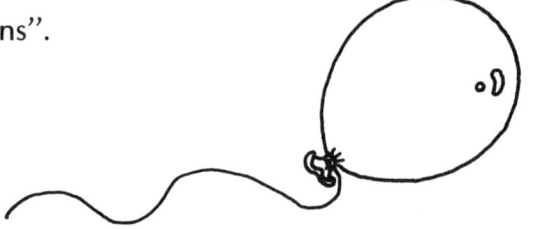

Learning Labs

★ Use balloons for the following science center experiments on static electricity:
1. Have children rub balloons with wool socks and stick them to walls.
2. Have children observe what happens when balloons are rubbed with wool socks and held over small pieces of paper.
3. Attach strings to two balloons. Have children observe what happens when the balloons are rubbed separately and then held near each other.

★ Use balloons for the following science center experiments on air:
1. Blow up balloons and let them go.
2. Blow up two balloons and attach one to each end of a yardstick. Balance the stick on a chair and have children observe what happens when one balloon is popped.

Think and Talk Time

★ Give each child an inflated balloon. Ask the children to use their senses to tell about the balloons. How does it feel? What does it look like? Does it have a smell? What noises can be made with it? How can the balloon be used?

★ Draw a geometric shape on the side of a uninflated balloon. Have the children predict what the shape will be when the balloon is inflated.

★ Read the poem to the children. Ask them to dramatize it using their balloons.

Project Pursuits

★ Make "Balloon Scatter Pictures." Have each child place a small amount of paint on a sheet of paper. Hand each child an inflated, untied balloon. Show the children how to use the air from the balloons to scatter the paint on the page. When dry, repeat the process using a different color. Display on a classroom wall.

★ Make "Funny-Face Balloon Puppets." Give each child an uninflated balloon. Ask the students to draw faces on their balloons with markers. Blow up the finished balloons and tie to close. Give each child a square of fabric with a hole cut out of the center. These are the puppet bodies. Tell the children to place the fabric over a hand and to hold the balloon faces through the hole. Ask the children to think of names for their puppets. Let them use the puppets for impromptu plays.

Movement Models

★ Give each child an inflated and tied balloon. Call out different body parts and ask the students to use those parts to keep their balloons in the air.

★ Give each child a balloon that is inflated and tied. Play music and let the children experiment with balloons, moving them in different ways. Encourage creativity. If you wish, turn the movements into a game of "Follow the Leader." Have one child perform an action with his or her balloon. The rest of the class should imitate the movement. Let everyone have a chance to be the leader.

★ Play "Balloon Stomp." Use string to fasten an inflated balloon to each child's ankle. Tell the students that when you give a certain signal they should try to stomp on another student's balloon while keeping their own from breaking. Emphasize safety rules before playing to keep this game from getting too rough. Divide the class into small groups before playing.

Balloon Day #2

Feature Focus Read the book or watch the film *The Red Balloon*.

Learning Labs

★ Have the children make "Red Balloon Snacks." Ask the children to shape premixed biscuit dough into balloon shapes. Have them paint the shapes red using egg yolk that has been diluted with water and mixed with red food coloring. Add stick pretzels for strings. Bake and eat for snacks.

Think and Talk Time

★ Read the book or show the film. Discuss the story with the children. What was unusual about the red balloon? What types of things did it see in the city? Discuss the children's experiences with balloons. What would it be like to have a balloon that behaves like the red balloon?

★ Show the class a large red helium balloon. Ask the children to describe what they would do with the balloon if it were theirs. Take the class outside and let the balloon go. Brainstorm with the children to create a list of places where the balloon might go. What types of places and things might it see?

Project Pursuits

★ Make individual balloon-shaped books for the class. For each child, cut two balloons out of red construction paper. Staple drawing paper inside the balloon shapes and trim to size. Have the children illustrate and write or dictate a story about the adventures of a red balloon on a farm, in a forest, or at a carnival. (If you wish, make this a class book with each child contributing a page.)

★ Cut out balloon shapes for the children to color. Supply different shades of red crayons or paints. Attach a piece of string to each shape. Have the children write or trace the word *red* on their balloons. Use the finished balloons for a bulletin board display.

Movement Models

★ Have children pretend to be red balloons flying around a city. Narrate a story as they move around the room. Ask them to pantomime different parts of the story. You might have them pretend to get caught in a tree, to be chased by a bird, and to fly in a window.

★ Play "Red Balloon Relay." Divide the class into teams. Mark a "turn-around" line some distance from the children. Ask the children to propel an inflated red balloon to the line and back again without touching the balloon. You might have them blow on the balloon, use a piece of cardboard to "fan" the balloon, or use a broom to sweep the balloon.

★ Make about twenty balloons from red construction paper. Divide the class into two groups. Tell one group to cover their eyes while the other group hides the balloons. Explain that the balloons must be hidden so that part of each one shows just a little. When they are all hidden, tell the other group to find them. Count to see that all twenty were found. Then reverse the roles of the group.

Balloon Day #3

Feature Focus Read the book *Hot Air Henry*.
Listen to the song "Up, Up & Away."

Learning Labs

★ Cut out hot-air balloon shapes from different colors of construction paper. Cut out the same number of balloon shapes from white drawing paper. For each colored balloon, write the corresponding color word on a white balloon. Pin both sets of balloons on a bulletin board. Ask the children to match the colored balloons with the color-word balloons.

★ Create a hot-air balloon role-playing area. Cut the tops off of large boxes and place the boxes in a drama area. Let the children pretend to take hot-air balloon rides.

Think and Talk Time

★ Discuss the book and the concepts of hot-air ballooning. Also talk about the colors of the balloons. Why might a balloonist want to use bright colors on his or her balloon? If possible, bring in pictures of balloon races to show the children.

★ Have the children close their eyes when they listen to the words and rhythm of the song. Discuss the places to which children might like to go in a hot-air balloon.

Project Pursuits

★ Have the children color hot-air balloon shapes on both sides with crayons or markers. Use yarn to tie the finished balloons onto berry baskets. Hang around the room as decorations.

★ Have the children draw pictures of things they might see if they were high up in the air in a balloon. Have each child write or dictate a few sentences about his or her picture. The comments should be written at the bottom of the pictures.

★ Have the children make "Hot-Air Balloon Pictures." Ask the children to mix blue tempera and liquid clothes starch on paper. Have them spread the mixture into interesting designs. While the paint dries, have the children draw, color, and cut out a hot-air balloon shape. Ask the students to glue the shape onto the finger-painted background. If you wish, place a photograph of each child's face in his or her balloon basket. Display on a classroom bulletin board.

Movement Models

★ Play "Keep It Up." Divide the class into small groups. Give each group an inflated balloon. Ask the children to hit the balloon back and forth to each other without letting it touch the floor. Have the children count the number of times they hit the balloons before they touch the floor.

★ Play a game called "Up, Up & Away." Set out as many carpet squares as there are children. Tell the children that these squares represent "landing spots." Ask the children to pretend to fly around the air in hot-air balloons when they hear music. When the music stops, they must fly to a landing spot. Only one child may be on a landing spot at a time. Each time you start the music again, remove one carpet square. Play until there are five or six squares left.

Box Days

Pattern Page

Box Days

Timing
  Near Christmas
  During an alphabet unit

What Children Bring
  Three boxes of any size.

Previous Day Reminder
  A square of construction paper with a bow and tag drawn on, pinned to each child's shirt. Tag reads "Bring three boxes, any size."

Ready Resources

Books
  Fischer, Leonard. *Boxes! Boxes!* New York: Viking-Penguin, 1984.
  Gauch, Patricia. *Christina Katerine and the Box.* New York: Putnam, 1980. (See related activities, page 16.)
  Maloney, Cecelia. *The Box Book.* Racine, WI: Western, 1978.
  McPhail, David. *The Cereal Box.* Boston: Little, Brown, 1974.
  Nixon, Joan. *The Secret Box Mystery.* New York: Putnam, 1974. (See related activities, page 18.)

Films
  BBC. *Boxes.* Paramus, NJ: Time-Life Films & Video, 1974.
  NBC. *How Do They Make Cardboard Boxes?* Chicago: Films, Inc., 1970. (See related activities, page 17.)

Poems
  Ridlon, Marci. "Johnny." In *Read-Aloud Rhymes for the Very Young.* Jack Prelutsky, ed. New York: Knopf, 1986.
  Silverstein, Shel. "Two Boxes." In *Where the Sidewalk Ends.* New York: Harper & Row, 1974.

Records and Songs
  Palmer, Hap. "Big Heavy Box." On *Pretend.* Educational Activities. (AR) 563. (See related activities, page 17.)

Box Day #1

Feature Focus   Read the book *Christina Katerine and the Box*.

Learning Labs

★ Place a large variety of big boxes in a creative drama area. Let the children pretend the boxes are trains, furniture, cars, forts, and so on.

★ Draw a series of pictures that show different sizes of boxes. Put each picture on a separate piece of paper. Have students sequence the pictures.

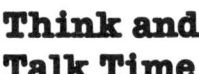

Think and Talk Time

★ Pick out one of the boxes brought by the children. (Try to choose one without a label.) Ask the class to think of different ways in which to use the box in a classroom, in a kitchen, in a playroom, and in a workshop.

★ Read the book to the children. Ask the class to suggest other things to do with a big box. Encourage creativity. What would they do with a box without a lid? With a box with holes in it? With a giant green box? With a small blue box? Keep a list of the children's suggestions.

★ Have the class tell a group "add-on" story about what happens to a box through its lifetime. Start with the lines, "There once was a big cardboard box. One day a little girl found the box and decided to turn it into a _____." Have each child, in turn, suggest another line of the story. Repeat all previous story lines before you ask for the next line.

Project Pursuits

★ Create a class book titled "Our Big Box Book." Have each child contribute a page. Ask the children to draw a picture of what they would do with a big box. Have the children write or dictate a few remarks about their drawings. Place the finished drawings inside a folded piece of construction paper. Write "Our Big Box Book" on the cover.

★ Obtain a large refrigerator or stove box from an appliance store. Explain to the class that you will help them turn the box into something else. Ask the class to choose one of the ideas from the list created during *Think and Talk Time*. Help turn the box into that object.

★ Divide the class into groups of two or three. Each group uses the assortment of boxes they brought from home, scrap paper, and fabric to create a box sculpture. Ask the children to glue the boxes together, then paint and decorate. Stress the fact that the creation does not have to look like anything in particular.

Movement Models

★ Have the children play "Box Tag." Scatter open boxes around the room. Choose one child to be IT. Tell the class that the boxes are "safe areas," but they have to have at least one foot in the box to be safe. At a given signal, IT chases the other children, trying to tag them. If a child is tagged, he or she must leave the game and sit by you. Continue until a specified number of children are out of the game. Then begin a new game with a new IT.

★ Play "Box-in-a-Box Relay." Divide the children into relay teams of equal numbers. Give each child a small empty box. Place a large empty box an equal distance from each team. Tell the children to run to the box, drop in the small box, then run back and tap the next player. Reverse the race by having the children run to the box and bring back the small boxes.

Box Day #2

Feature Focus Watch the film *How Do They Make Cardboard Boxes?* Listen to the song "Big Heavy Box."

Learning Labs

★ Make a "Box City" role-playing area. Cover individual milk cartons (which have been rinsed and dried) with white paper. Decorate, or have the children decorate, the cartons to look like buildings. Use creased paper for roofs. Place the carton buildings on a large piece of fabric that has been marked with streets and roads. Add small plastic cars, trucks, and airplanes to the city. Let children use their imaginations to create a name for the city and its inhabitants.

★ Put a variety of small boxes on a table in a learning area. Ask children to fit smaller boxes inside of larger boxes so the fewest number of boxes are visible.

Think and Talk Time

★ Discuss the movie. Then have the class classify the cardboard boxes they brought from home by use. For example, the boxes could be put into groups of cereal boxes, shoe boxes, gift boxes, and so on. Ask children why boxes that are used for the same purpose are sometimes different sizes.

Project Pursuits

★ Have the children make "Scoop Ball Sets." Give each child an individual milk carton that has the bottom cut out. Have the children crumple newspaper into tight balls about the size of a Ping-Pong ball. Tape a piece of string onto each ball. Then tape the other end of the string inside each carton. The ball should be outside the carton. To play, children hold the milk carton (open bottom facing upwards) by the "handle" (the spout) of the carton. Tell students that they should "scoop" the ball into the carton.

★ Let the children use the bottom six inches of half-gallon milk cartons to make "Special Boxes." Cut off the milk carton bottoms, and help the children cover the carton with white paper. Have the children decorate the outside with pictures cut from magazines, torn pieces of tissue paper, finger paints, or crayon drawings. Laminate the finished products with clear Con-Tact paper.

Movement Models

★ Play the song. Have children pretend to carry (or push) heavy boxes across the room in time to the music.

★ Let the children play with their scoop-ball sets from *Project Pursuits*.

★ Cut cardboard boxes into 12" square pieces. Give each child a square. Have the children place the cardboard squares in front of them on the floor. Then give directions for movements relative to the "box." For example, you might say, "Jump into the box," "Jump out of the box," "Jump over the box," "Hop around the box," and "Crawl over the box." Ask the children to think of other movements they can do in relation to the box.

Box Day #3

Feature Focus   Read the book *The Secret Box Mystery*.

Learning Labs

★ Make a "Feeling Box." Tape down the top of a box and cut out a hole on one side. Staple a sock cuff or a piece of cloth over the hole so children can reach inside without seeing in. Place an object inside the box. Have children guess what the object is just by feeling it. Repeat using different objects.

Think and Talk Time

★ Before class, place a gift for the students inside a box and wrap up the box. Put a label on the box that reads "Don't Open This Box." Talk to the students about the tag. What might be inside box? Have the class brainstorm to create a list of possibilities.

★ Show the children some other gift-wrapped boxes. Help the students discover what is inside each box by answering yes and no questions posed by the class.

★ Read the book. Stop at the point where Paul describes what is missing from the secret box. Ask the students to draw pictures of what they think is inside the box. Reread the description if necessary. After all the students have finished their drawings, finish the story. Ask the children if they were surprised by the thing inside the box.

Project Pursuits

★ Have the children draw pictures of what they think is inside the box you brought. Place the finished pictures on a bulletin board under the caption "What's Inside?" At the end of the day, open the wrapped box for the children and give them the surprise.

★ Have the children make a "Jack or Jill in the Box." Have each child decorate a small box using pieces of tissue paper or construction paper. Have each child make a "Jack" or "Jill" by drawing a face on a construction paper shape. Have the children glue the face to a tongue depressor. Let them add hair and other features using markers and materials from the scrap or junk box. Help each child cut a small hole, just big enough for the puppet handle, in the bottom of his or her box. Push the tongue depressor through the hole. Children can manipulate the puppet by moving the handle.

Movement Models

★ Play a game called "Who Is in the Box?" Ask the children to sit in a circle. Choose one child to leave the room. Choose another child to hide "in the box" (this can be somewhere out of sight in the room). Have the children in the circle rearrange themselves so the empty spot is not noticeable. Tell the child waiting outside to return and ask him or her to identify the child "in the box." Give all the children a chance to be inside the box and the child to guess.

★ Set up a "Box Obstacle Course." Set large and small boxes in random order around a large open area. Mark off a path that twists around the boxes for the children to follow. Ask the children to perform different movements as they follow the path. Some movements you might call for are skipping, hopping on one foot, bouncing a ball, or doing a crab walk.

Clown Days

Pattern Page

Clown Days

Timing
　　When a circus comes to town
　　Circus Week (8/1)

What Children Wear
　　Clown makeup or a clown costume.

Previous Day Reminder
　　A red stick-on dot on each child's nose.

Special Speaker
　　If possible, have a local clown come in and demonstrate how to put on the makeup and costume. (This helps students realize that clowns are real people.)

Ready Resources

Books
　　Adler, David A. *You Think It's Fun to Be a Clown?* New York: Doubleday, 1980. (See related activities, page 24.)
　　Coleman, Sheila. *McHappy, The Unhappy Clown.* Nashville, TN: Nelson, 1986.
　　Johnson, Sharon. *I Want to Be a Clown.* Grand Haven, MI: School Zone Publishing, 1986.
　　Pellowski, Michael. *Clara Joins the Circus.* New York: Parents Magazine Press, 1981.
　　Quackenbush, Robert. *The Man on the Flying Trapeze: The Circus Life of Emmet Kelly, Sr.* Philadelphia: Lippencott, 1975.
　　Sobel, Harriet. *Clowns.* New York: Harper & Row, 1982.
　　Thaler, Mike. *The Clown's Smile.* New York: Harper & Row, 1986.

Films
　　ABC. *Clowns, The Laugh Makers.* Chicago: Encyclopedia Britannica Educational Corporation, 1977. (See related activities, page 23.)
　　Arthur Gold Productions. *Clowns Are for Laughing.* Santa Monica, CA: Pyramid Film & Video, 1973.

Poems
　　Hopkins, Lee B. "The Clown." In *Circus! Circus!* New York: Knopf, 1982.
　　Scott, Louise B. "Floppety Clown." In *Rhymes for Learning Times.* Minneapolis, MN: Denison, 1984.

Records and Songs
　　Palmer, Hap. "The Clown." On *Pretend.* Educational Activities. (AR) 563. (See related activities, page 22.)
　　Wagner, Laverne, and Paulette Berry. "Funny Little Clown." In *Tunes for Tots.* Carthage, IL: Good Apple, 1982.

Short Stories
　　Ward, Winifred. "The Clown Who Forgot How to Laugh." In *Stories to Dramatize.* New Orleans, LA: Anchorage Press, 1952.

Teacher Resources
　　Stolzenberg, Mark. *Clowns for Circus and Stage.* New York: Sterling, 1983. (See related activities, page 22.)

Clown Day #1

Feature Focus   Listen to the song "The Clown."
Use the resource *Clowns for Circus and Stage*.

Learning Labs

★ Make a blank clown face for a flannel board. Provide several different sizes and colors of felt geometric shapes. Encourage the children to make silly clowns using the felt shapes for facial features.

★ Make a clown with raised arms out of construction paper. Place on a bulletin board. Cut circles out of paper and on each circle write a numeral, 1–10. Have the students put the circles in numerical order between the clown's arms. Pin the caption, "Help the clown juggle the balls" on top of the board.

★ Place clown costumes and toys in a creative play area. Let children pretend to be clowns in a circus.

Think and Talk Time

★ Discuss clowns with the class. What are they like? What do they do? Start the discussion by asking questions such as, "Have any of you ever seen a clown?" "What type of stunts did the clown do?" "What makes a clown funny?"

★ Listen to the song. Then have children tell a group story about a small clown who wants to join the circus. What types of tricks does the clown do? Why does the clown want to join the circus? Does the clown have a happy face or a sad face?

Project Pursuits

★ Have the children make "Life-size Clowns." Draw around each child onto a piece of large butcher paper. (You might have children do this in pairs.) Have the children paint in the details of the faces and costumes. Ask the children to name their clowns. Display on the walls the caption, "The Parade of Classroom Clowns," or "If I Joined the Circus."

★ Play a game called "The Clown's Hats." Make a 9" × 12" card for each child. On each card, draw a clown face and a set of six hats. Print a color word you are teaching on each hat. Use different color words on each card. Cut out colored paper hats to match all the color words. Place these within reach of the children. Prepare a spinner with the color words in sections around it. Have the children take turns spinning the spinner, reading the word it lands on, and looking at their sets of hats for the word. If they find it, they cover it with the appropriately colored paper hat.

Movement Models

★ Use the resource book as a guide for teaching students simple clown stunts, such as somersaults, duck walking, and tightrope walking (on the floor or balance beam). Have students practice the stunts. Then let the children go on a parade to other classrooms to show off their costumes and stunts.

★ Ask the children to play a variation of "Follow the Leader." Choose one child to be the leader. Have the child perform silly actions, such as pretending to be a monkey. The rest of the children must copy the movement. Give each child a chance to be a leader.

Clown Day #2

Feature Focus   Watch the film *Clowns, The Laugh Makers.*

Learning Labs

★ Make "Clown Salad" with the children. Serve each child two peach or apricot halves. Show them how to arrange the fruits on a plate to form a face and a body. Provide thin celery or carrot sticks for legs and arms. Ask the children to make faces on the top peach or apricot section using raisins for eyes and a cherry half for a nose. Use grated cheese or cottage cheese for hair.

Think and Talk Time

★ Show the film. Ask the children to compare clown school to their own school. How is it different? How is it the same?

★ Discuss what it would be like if people other than clowns wore clown costumes at their jobs. For example, you might discuss what would happen if a teacher, a mother, a librarian, a police officer, and a doctor wore clown costumes to work. When would it be a good idea to wear a costume? When would it be a bad idea?

Project Pursuits

★ Have the students make body puppets. Have each child draw a clown face on a paper plate. Attach each plate to a 12" × 15" piece of cardboard. Make arms for the cardboard body from 3"-wide strips of cloth cut to the length of each child's arms. Attach one end of the arms to each "shoulder" of the body. Attach a rubber band to the free end of each arm by folding and sewing the fabric over part of the band. Attach the center of a 2¼' length of ribbon to the top of each plate. To wear the puppet, tie the ribbon around the child's neck and slip the rubber bands over the child's wrists. The child can manipulate the arms of the puppet by moving his or her arms. If you wish, add fabric ruffles and other decorations to the clown.

Movement Models

★ Narrate a story about clowns in a circus. Have the children pantomime actions as you tell the story.

★ Divide the class into groups of two. Ask each group to work on some clown stunts to share with the rest of the class. Supply the children with props, such as balance beams, large boxes, balls, old hats, and jump ropes.

★ Play a game called "It's Circus Time!" Choose one child to be the ringmaster and another to be the head clown. All the other children are clowns. Tell all the clowns to stand on a line about 30 feet away from where the ringmaster is standing. The head clown leads the other clowns to the ringmaster and asks, "What time is it, ringmaster?" The ringmaster answers different times. If the ringmaster says, "It's Circus Time," the clowns run away. The ringmaster tries to catch them by tagging them on the shoulder. Anyone the ringmaster tags must help the ringmaster catch the remaining clowns.

Clown Day #3

Feature Focus  Read the book *You Think It's Fun to Be a Clown?*

Learning Labs

★ Let the children turn upside-down ice-cream cones into clowns. Have them use frosting to make pom-poms on the cone "hat" and facial freatures on the ice-cream "face." Eat for snacks.

★ Provide students with bright colors of paint in the art center. Encourage students to paint clowns. Record a few dictated remarks about each child's painting.

★ Draw clown faces on pieces of cardboard. Give each clown a circular nose. Inside each nose write a lower-case letter. Cut out red construction-paper circles that are the same size as the clowns' noses. Write the corresponding capital letters inside the circles. Leave in a learning area. Have students place each capital letter nose on the corresponding lower-case letter.

Think and Talk Time

★ Read the book to the children. Discuss the disadvantages of being a clown that the author lists. Brainstorm with the children to create a list that tells other disadvantages of being a clown. Also create a list with the children that tells advantages of being a clown.

★ Make up imaginary situations and have the students tell what they would say or do if these things really happened to them. For example, "What would you do if you woke up one morning and found you had a clown's nose instead of your own?"

Project Pursuits

★ Have the children make a class bulletin board. Ask each child to make a part of a clown out of large sheets of construction paper. Put the separate pieces together on a wall or bulletin board. The crazier it turns out, the better. Title the creation, "Just Clowning Around."

★ Have the children make a class book titled, "Being A Clown." Ask each child to draw a picture of something good or bad that happens to a clown. Have each child write or dictate a few sentences about his or her picture. The sentences should be written at the bottom of the picture. Place the pictures inside a piece of folded construction paper. Write the title on the cover.

★ Supply the children with burlap, colorful yarns, and large-eyed blunt needles. Help the children use a running stitch to outline a clown's face on the fabric.

Movement Models

★ Have the children pantomime a clown who is feeling afraid, excited, nervous, clumsy, shy, and happy. If you wish, write each feeling on a card. Have the children sit in a circle and choose one child to act out a feeling. The child picks one of the cards and acts out the feeling. The other children try to guess which feeling the child is acting out. Let each child have a chance to pantomime while the other children guess.

★ Play "Be a Clown Relay." Divide the class into teams. Mark off a goal line some distance from the children. Each child has to run to the goal line and put on a big shirt, big pants, big shoes, and a big hat. The child then jumps into the box which contained the clothes, jumps back out, removes the clothes, and runs back to tag the next runner in line.

Cookie Days

Pattern Page

Cookie Days

Timing
  Cookie Monster's Birthday (11/10)
  Gloomy Winter Day

Previous Day Preview
  If you are doing the unit on Cookie Monster's Birthday, tell the class that someone very special is having a birthday the next day.

Ready Resources

Books
  Carlson, Ann. *The Cookie Looker.* Lynnwood, WA: Karwyn, 1983.
  Daly, Niki. *Ben's Gingerbread Man.* New York: Viking-Penguin, 1985.
  Galdone, Paul. *The Gingerbread Boy.* Boston: Houghton Mifflin, 1975.
  Hillert, Margaret. *The Cookie House.* Cleveland, OH: Follet, 1978.
  _____. *The Little Cookie.* Cleveland, OH: Modern Curriculum Press, 1980.
  Korr, David. *Cookie Monster and the Cookie Tree.* Racine, WI: Western, 1977. (See related activities, page 28.)
  Numeroff, Laura J. *If You Give a Mouse a Cookie.* New York: Harper & Row, 1985. (See related activities, page 30.)
  Sesame Street. *Cookie Monster's Book of Cookie Shapes.* Racine, WI: Western, 1979. (See related activities, page 28.)

Poems
  Anderson, Paul S. "The Cookie Jar People." In *Story Telling with the Flannel Board,* Book 2. Minneapolis, MN: Denison, 1970.

Records and Songs
  Beall, Pamela C., and Susan H. Nipp. "Who Stole the Cookies from the Cookie Jar?" In *Wee Sing and Play.* Los Angeles: Price, Stern, Sloan, 1983. (See related activities, page 29.)
  C Is for Cookie. Sesame Street Records. (SSR) 22058.
  Sharon, Lois, and Bram. "Cookie Jar." On *One Elephant, Deux Elephants.* Elephant Records. (LFN) 7801.
  Wayman, Joe, and Don Mitchell. "Cookies, Cookies, Cookies." On *Dandy-Lions Never Roar.* Good Apple. (GA) 47. (See related activities, page 29.)

Cookie Day #1

Feature Focus Read the book *Cookie Monster and the Cookie Tree*. Have children look at the book *Cookie Monster's Book of Cookie Shapes*.

Learning Labs

★ Have the children make "Cookie Monster Cupcakes." Remove the paper from baked cupcakes. Have the children turn the cupcakes upside down and frost them with blue frosting for fur. Let them add mini-marshmallows for eyes (use dots of black frosting for pupils).

★ Let students use blue, white, and black paint to paint pictures of Cookie Monster in the art area.

Think and Talk Time

★ Discuss Cookie Monster. Ask students to pantomime how he eats cookies. Discuss this method of eating and ask students what would be a more acceptable way to eat cookies.

★ Guide children into a discussion about nutrition. Ask them questions such as "Does Cookie Monster eat anything except cookies?" "How do you know?" "What would happen if we just ate cookies?" "What things must we eat to stay healthy?"

★ Have the class tell a group "add-on" story about Cookie Monster's Birthday. Start with the lines, "Today is Cookie Monster's Birthday. He wants to celebrate with a _____." Have each child suggest a way in which Cookie Monster could celebrate his birthday. Repeat all previous ideas before you ask for the next one.

Project Pursuits

★ Have each child create one page for a class book. Ask the children to draw pictures showing something that Cookie Monster might do on his birthday. Ask each child to write or dictate a few comments about his or her picture. Place the finished pictures inside a piece of folded construction paper and write "Cookie Monster's Birthday" on the cover.

★ Have the children make "Cookie Monster Puppets." Ask each student to glue a strip of blue fake fur (available in craft stores) onto a tongue depressor or a wood stick. Add blue pom-poms for heads. Help the children glue two white beads on each pom-pom for eyes. Use the stick puppets for a puppet show about Cookie Monster.

★ Provide the children with different colors of playdough. Ask them to make cookies for Cookie Monster. Have them use different tools and make different shapes of cookies.

Movement Models

★ Play a game called "Feed Cookie Monster." Cut out blue construction paper into a Cookie Monster shape. Glue to tagboard. Add two white circles with black dots in the middle for eyes and a large white circle for a mouth. Make several paper cookies out of brown paper. Choose one child to start the game. Blindfold the child and turn him or her around and around. Then have the child try to pin the cookie as close to Cookie Monster's mouth as he or she can. Let all the children have a chance to "feed Cookie Monster."

★ Play "Sit on a Cookie." Set out butcher-paper "giant cookies" for all but one of the children in the class. The extra child is the baker. Ask the children to sit on their cookies while the baker stands. The baker says, "Where are my cookies? I know I had one. Where are my cookies? You'd better run!" On the word *run*, all the children run to another cookie while the baker also tries to sit on a cookie. The child left without a cookie is the next baker.

Cookie Day #2

Feature Focus Listen to the song "Cookies, Cookies, Cookies." Sing the song "Who Stole the Cookies from the Cookie Jar?"

Learning Labs

★ Cut out circles from tan contruction paper to represent cookies. On each circle draw one to ten black circles to represent chips. Write each corresponding numeral on a small paper plate. Have the students count the number of "chips" in each cookie and place the cookie on the correct plate. To make this activity self-checking, place matching stick-on dots on the back of the plate and on the cookies for that plate.

★ Make a cookie-puzzle game by drawing around a cookie cutter onto tan construction paper. Cut out the shapes, then cut the shapes into irregular pieces to make puzzle pieces. Leave in a learning center for the children to put together.

Think and Talk Time

★ Listen to "Cookies, Cookies, Cookies." Ask the children if they think it's possible to eat cookies without creating crumbs. Discuss their answers. Then give each child a chocolate-chip cookie. Ask them to count the number of chips in their cookies. After the chips have been counted, let the children eat their cookies while leaning over paper napkins. Ask them to check for crumbs. Could they eat their cookies without crumbs?

Project Pursuits

★ Show students a graph and explain what it is. Tell the class that they are going to help you graph favorite cookies. Brainstorm with the class to create a list of different types of cookies. Then have the students vote on their favorite cookies. Ask all the children who like the same type of cookie to stand in a line. Point out that the students have created a "body graph." Count and compare the number of students in each line. Create a chart graph from the information.

★ Have the class create a "Cookie Cookbook." Ask each child to dictate the recipe for his or her favorite cookie. You should record the information and the procedure verbatim. Ask a volunteer to type up the recipes. Encourage each child to illustrate his or her entry. Duplicate and send home as a gift for parents.

★ Have children make "cookies" out of play-dough and cookie cutters. Let them use 1"-diameter dowels for rolling pins.

Movement Models

★ Sing and play the singing game "Who Stole the Cookies from the Cookie Jar?"

★ Play "Put the Chocolate Chip in the Cookie." Tape a large piece of paper on the floor. Draw four or five large circles on it. In each circle, write a numeral. Explain to the children that these circles represent cookies. Let the children take turns tossing "chocolate chips" (brown beanbags) into the circles. Tell the children to keep track of the points they get by counting out mini-chocolate chips. At the end of the game, ask all the children to count their chips. Let the children eat the chips as an after-game treat.

Cookie Day #3

Feature Focus Read the book *If You Gave a Mouse a Cookie*.

Learning Labs

★ Make "Cookie Mice" with the class. Have each child cut out two small circles and one large circle from premixed cookie dough. Show the children how to arrange the pieces on a cookie sheet to form a mouse head and ears. Let the children add raisin eyes and a nut or raisin nose. Whiskers can be made from small pretzel sticks. Bake and eat while reading the story.

★ Leave gray, brown, and beige finger paint in an art area. Have the children paint pictures of mice eating cookies.

Think and Talk Time

★ Read the book to the children. Ask the children to look closely at several illustrations of the boy and the mouse. Ask them to suggest different things that the boy might be saying to himself as he helps the mouse. What is the mouse saying to himself? Reread the last page of the story. Ask the children to describe what they think will happen next. Role-play some possible actions.

Project Pursuits

★ Let the children make "Mouse Puppets." Have each child roll a piece of 2" × 3" oak tag into a cylinder. This is the finger holder. Next, have each child stuff a 6" square of gray fabric with tissue paper or old stockings. Help the child slip the stuffed cloth over the top of the oak tag cylinder as shown. Secure with a rubber band. Ask the children to make ears and facial features out of construction paper. Glue in place.

★ Have the children make "Hidden Cookie Pictures." Show the children how circles (cookies) can be turned into different objects, such as wheels, flowers, eyes, and so on. Ask the students to draw pictures using as many circles as possible. It would be helpful to provide templates of different-sized circles.

Movement Models

★ Divide the class into groups of two. Retell the story and have the children pantomime the actions. One child in each group should be the mouse while the other should be the boy. Read again, and let the children switch roles.

★ Play a game called "Give the Mouse a Cookie." Ask the children to sit in a circle on the floor. Give them a large brown yarn ball. Teach them to say, "I'm giving _____ (child's name) mouse a cookie." The child holding the ball should say the sentence and then roll the ball to the child that he or she names. Encourage the children to give everyone a turn. After a round of rolling the ball, ask the children to stand up and toss the ball to each other.

Dot Days

Pattern Page

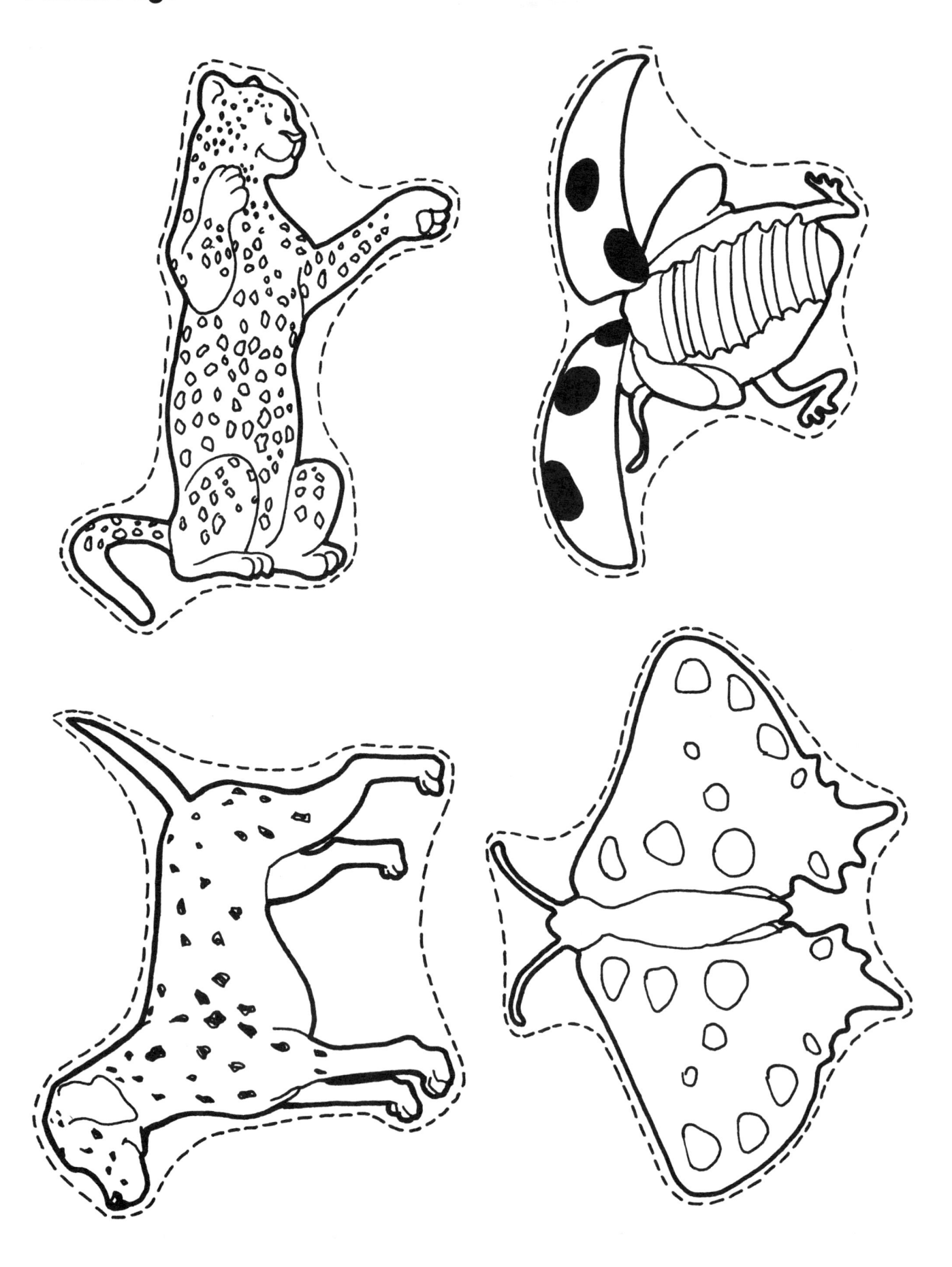

32

Dot Days

Timing
　　Anytime

What Children Bring
　　Something with dots or spots.

Previous Day Reminder
　　A stick-on dot on the back of each child's hand.

Ready Resources

Books

　　Bonsall, Crosby N. *What Spot?* New York: Harper & Row, 1963.
　　Devlin, Wende, and Harry Devlin. *Old Witch and the Polka-Dot Ribbon.* New York: Scholastic, 1980. (See related activities, page 34.)
　　Galbraith, Kathryn O. *Spots Are Special.* New York: Atheneum, 1976. (See related activities, page 35.)
　　Kumin, Maxine. *What Color Is Caeser?* New York: McGraw-Hill, 1978.
　　Levitin, Sonia. *A Single Speckled Egg.* Boston: Parnassus Press, 1976.
　　Lopshire, Robert. *Put Me in the Zoo.* New York: Random House, 1960. (See related activities, page 36.)
　　Slobodkin, Louis. *The Polka-Dot Goat.* New York: Macmillan, 1964.

Records and Songs

　　Stephens, Dodie. "Tan Shoes and Pink Shoelaces." On *Twenty-Four Greatest Dumb Ditties.* K-Tel. 9330.

Short Stories

　　Carlson, Natalie. "Speckled Hen's Egg." In *The Talking Cat and Other Stories of French Canada.* New York: Harper & Row, 1952.

Dot Day #1

Feature Focus   Read the book *Old Witch and the Polka-Dot Ribbon*.

Learning Labs

★ Glue several library card pockets to the inside of a file folder. On each pocket make a different polka-dot design. Draw the same designs on paper geometric shapes. Ask students to place each shape in the corresponding pocket.

★ Leave dominoes in a creative play area. Let children match the dots on the different pieces.

★ Make edible "Polka-Dot Ribbons." Cut wheat bread into rectangular strips. Let each child spread cream cheese or peanut butter on a strip. Have them add "polka dots" using raisins. Eat for snacks.

Think and Talk Time

★ Have the children share the dotted or spotted items they brought from home. After the items have been displayed, ask the children to arrange them according to the size of the dots on the objects.

★ Read the book to the children. Why did the witch win a polka-dot ribbon? Brainstorm with the children to create a list of other things people could do to win polka-dot ribbons. Ask the children to tell stories about what they would like to do to win a ribbon.

Project Pursuits

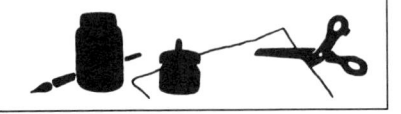

★ Create a class book titled "Our Polka-Dot Ribbon Awards." Ask each child to contribute a picture that shows someone doing something to earn a polka-dot ribbon. Have each child write or dictate a story about the picture. Place the final work inside a piece of folded construction paper that has been covered with stick-on dots. Write the title on the cover.

★ Let the children create their own dot-to-dot pictures. Have each child draw or stick on different colored dots on a sheet of paper. After they have completed this task, ask them to connect the dots using corresponding colors. If you wish, have children exchange papers before they connect the dots.

★ Give each child a piece of polka-dot ribbon to make into an award. Let them use scrap materials for decoration.

Movement Models

★ Dramatize an award ceremony. Ask each child to present the award he or she made in *Project Pursuits* to another child in the class. Have the children explain what is special about the person receiving the award.

★ Play a game called "The Polka-Dot Award." Ask the children to form a single-file line holding on to each other's waists. Tuck a piece of polka-dot ribbon into the waistband of the last child in line. The first person in line tries to take the ribbon by maneuvering the line around. After the ribbon is taken, the first child in line goes to the rear of the line and wears the ribbon. If your class is large, divide it in half to play this game.

Dot Day #2

Feature Focus   Read the book *Spots are Special*.

Learning Labs

★ Cut out shapes of spotted animals from construction paper. On each shape write a numeral. Laminate with clear Con-Tact paper. Leave the animals and small stick-on dots in a learning area. Have students stick the correct number of "spots" on each animal shape. When finished, they can pull off dots and use again.

Think and Talk Time

★ Ask the children if any of them have ever had chicken pox. Discuss what it is like to have the disease and what the children did while they were sick. After the discussion, read the book to the children. Discuss how the children in the book overcame the boredom of being sick. Why were the "spots" special?

★ Brainstorm with the children to create a list of other spotted animals or spotted things the children could be. Have the children tell stories about what they would do and where they would live if they were these spotted things.

Project Pursuits

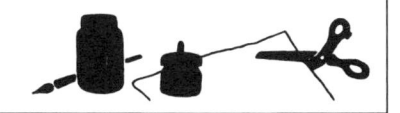

★ Have the children create a class book. Let each child draw a picture of himself or herself as an animal or thing with spots. Ask each child to write or dictate a short story about what it is like to have spots. Put the finished pages inside a folded piece of construction paper. Title the book "Our Spots."

★ Ask the children to pretend that a friend has chicken pox. Supply the children with crayons, markers, fabric, lace, paper, and other materials to make get-well cards for these imaginary friends. Ask each child to write or dictate a line telling his or her friend why spots are special. These lines should be written inside the finished cards. Display on a bulletin board or wall.

Movement Models

★ Let the children pretend to be different spotted animals. Ask them to move around the room in time to music.

★ Play "Don't Step on the Spots." Tape large paper circles to the play area floor. Mark off two goal lines. Have the children stand behind one line. Ask them to run to the opposite line and back again without stepping on a spot. If a child does step on a spot, he or she must circle around the spot before continuing.

★ Teach the children how to play "Spot Tag." Ask the children to scatter themselves around the play area. Choose one child to be IT. When IT tags a child, that child must place his or her hand on the "spot" that IT touched. Then the tagged child tries to tag other children with his or her free hand. Play the game again once most of the children have been tagged.

Dot Day #3

Feature Focus Read the book *Put Me in the Zoo*.

Learning Labs

★ Place paints in the creative arts area. Let the children paint dotted animals on colored construction paper.

★ Teach the children how to play tiddlywinks. Call the pieces "hopping dots."

★ Leave rubber "dot" stamps and ink pads in a learning area. Have children stamp out spots in time to music.

Think and Talk Time

★ Discuss the difference between dots and spots. Brainstorm with the children to create a list of places where they have seen spots and dots. Ask the children if dots can be spots. Can spots be dots?

★ Read the book to the class. Discuss why the animal with dots wanted to be put in a zoo. What kind of animal was the animal in the story? Have the children name the animal.

★ Compare a circus and a zoo. Why was the circus a better place for the dotted animal? Ask the children which trick they liked best and why. Have them suggest other tricks that the animal might do.

Project Pursuits

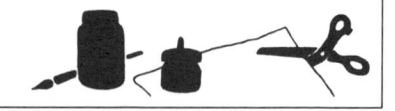

★ Have the children create a "Dotted Creature." Divide the class into groups of four. Each child in the group creates a body part, such as a body, a head, legs, and a tail, out of construction paper. Encourage the children to make the pieces large, and ask them not to look at what the other children are making. Let the children add large dots using markers or crayons. Glue each group's animal parts together on a large piece of white paper. Have the children add in background that shows what the creature eats, where it lives, and any other similar "facts." Display the final projects on a wall under the caption, "Put Us in the Zoo."

★ Let the children make spotted animals out of contrasting colors of playdough. Have each child write or dictate a story about his or her creature.

Movement Models

★ Play "Pin the Spot on the Dot." Draw an animal shape on a large piece of construction paper. Draw several large "dots" on the animal. Let blindfolded students try to pin construction paper "spots" on the dots. Let all the children have a chance to play.

★ Let the children pretend to be different dotted animals doing tricks. Have the children use their imaginations to create the tricks they perform.

★ Play "The Dot Game." Place a carpet square or chair in the play area for every child in the class except one. Choose one child to be IT. Give the rest of the children colored construction-paper circles. IT stands in the middle of the area and calls out a color. All the children holding that color of dot must change places while IT tries to steal an empty chair. The child left without a seat becomes the next IT.

Dragon Days

Pattern Page

38

Dragon Days

Timing
    Chinese New Year
    During an alphabet unit

Morning Preview
    Before class, make dragon puzzles by gluing pictures of dragons onto cardboard and cutting the dried pictures into puzzle pieces. When students arrive, divide them into groups of three and have each group work on a puzzle.

Ready Resources

Books

De Paola, Tomie. *The Knight and the Dragon.* New York: Putnam. 1980. (See related activities, page 41.)

Gannett, Ruth. *My Father's Dragon.* New York: Random House, 1948.

Jones, Maurice. *I'm Going on a Dragon Hunt.* New York: Scholastic, 1987. (See related activities, page 40.)

Kent, Jack. *The Once-Upon-A-Time Dragon.* San Diego, CA: Harcourt Brace Jovanovich, 1982.

_____. *There's No Such Thing as a Dragon.* Racine, WI: Western, 1975.

Konopka, Ursula, and Josef Guggenmos. *Dragon Franz.* New York: Greenwillow Books, 1977.

Manushkin, Fran. *Moon Dragon.* New York: Macmillan, 1982.

Muller, Romeo. *Puff the Magic Dragon.* New York: Avon Books, 1979.

Timm, Stephen. *The Dragon and the Mouse.* Fargo, ND: Touchstone Enterprises, 1981.

Williams, Jay. *Everyone Knows What a Dragon Looks Like.* New York: Scholastic, 1979.

Films

Alphabet Dragon. New York: BFA Educational Media, 1979.

Dragon Stew. New York: BFA Educational Media, 1972. (See related activities, page 42.)

Screenscope. *Dragon in a Wagon.* Deerfield, IL: MTI Teleprograms, 1977.

Screenscope. *Jonathan and the Dragon.* Deerfield, IL: MTI Teleprograms, 1977.

Poems

Bennett, Rowena. "A Modern Dragon." In *Read-Aloud Rhymes for the Very Young.* Jack Prelutsky. New York: Knopf, 1984.

Kuskin, Karla. "The Gold Tinted Dragon." In *Read-Aloud Rhymes for the Very Young.* Jack Prelutsky. New York: Knopf, 1984.

Dragon Day #1

Feature Focus Read the book *I'm Going on a Dragon Hunt*.

Learning Labs

★ Leave dress-up items such as hats, gloves, toy butterfly nets, and toy shields in a creative play area. Let children pretend they are searching for dragons.

★ Draw several different pairs of dragons on green construction paper. Cut out and let children find the matching pairs.

Think and Talk Time

★ Before reading the book, discuss dragons with the children. Would a dragon make a good pet? Why or why not? Display pictures of dragons from various books. Have the children compare the drawings. What makes a beast a dragon?

★ Ask the children to think about going on a dragon hunt. Ask them questions such as, "Where would you look for a dragon?" "How would you catch the dragon?" "Where would you keep the dragon once it was caught?" "How might a dragon help you?" After the discussion, read the book to the children. What types of places does the main character go through to get to the dragon's cave? What happens once he reaches the cave?

Project Pursuits

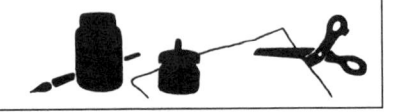

★ Have the class make a book titled, "We Went on a Dragon Hunt." Ask each child to draw a picture of a pet dragon. Encourage the students to include themselves in the pictures. Also ask them to draw in backgrounds. Have each child write or dictate a few sentences about how and where he or she caught the dragon, where it will be kept, or any other information about the dragon the child wants to share. Place the pictures and writing inside a piece of folded green construction paper, staple, and write the title on the cover.

★ Ask each child to draw an outline of a dragon on a large piece of paper. Show the children how to make "dragon scales" by gluing pieces of green tissue paper inside the dragon outline. Have the children add buttons or beans for eyes and pieces of red construction ribbon or yarn for flame. Ask the children to add a background and to name their dragons.

Movement Models

★ Play a game called "Dragon Hunt." Ask the children to pretend that they must find a large, green dragon, who is living in a cave. Choose one child to be the dragon. Have the rest of the children close their eyes while the dragon hides somewhere in the play area. When you call out, "Let's go on a dragon hunt!" the children open their eyes and search for the dragon. When they find the dragon, they must run back to a designated "castle" or safe area. The dragon tries to catch someone who will be the dragon for the next game.

★ Make about twenty circles from green construction paper. Call these circles dragons. Divide the class into two teams. Tell one group to cover their eyes while the other group hides the dragons. Explain that the dragons must be hidden so a little part of each dragon still shows. When all the dragons are hidden, tell the other group to find them. Count to see that all were found, then reverse the roles of the groups.

Dragon Day #2

Feature Focus Read the book *The Knight and the Dragon*.

Learning Labs

★ Create two settings in a drama area—a castle and a cave. Crowns, capes, fake rocks, and blankets can be added for atmosphere.

★ Encourage the students to paint pictures of dragons. Let the students use markers to add scales and details when the paintings are dry.

Think and Talk Time

★ Ask the children if they have ever read or heard stories about knights fighting with dragons. Discuss the usual settings of these dragon stories. Why do kings and princes always want to get rid of the dragons in their kingdoms? What usually happens to the dragon? Read the book to the class. Compare the story to other stories about knights and dragons. Why did the knight and dragon feel they must fight each other? What did they do to get ready for the fight? What happened during the fight? At the end of the fight?

Project Pursuits

★ Build a dragon with the class. Give each child a paper plate to decorate for a scale on a large dragon. Assemble the dragon on a classroom wall or bulletin board. Add a dragon face that has fire coming out of the nostrils. Ask the children to choose a name for the dragon. Then have the children dictate stories about the dragon.

★ Have the children make "Knight Puppets." Give each child two paper plates. Ask the children to cut off the bottom third of one plate. Help the children staple the edges of the two plates together, leaving the bottom open. The plates should form a "glove" as shown. Have the children make a knight face and helmet on the front of the puppet with aluminum foil, feathers, scrap paper, and fabric. If you wish, children can add construction-paper arms, legs, and body. Let the children use their puppets to create impromptu plays about knights.

Movement Models

★ Play a game called "Knights and Dragons." Divide the class into two teams on opposite goal lines facing each other. Call one team the knights and the other team the dragons. Ask the dragons to turn their backs to the knights. Then tell the knights to tiptoe up to the dragons very quietly. When you call out, "The knights are coming!" the dragons turn around and chase the knights back to the knights' goal line. Tagged players become part of the dragon team. Play again, reversing the roles.

★ Have the children pretend to be knights off to hunt a dragon. Teach them the following song (tune of "A-Hunting We Will Go"):
   Dragon hunting we will go,
   Dragon hunting we will go,
   We'll catch a dragon and
   put it in our wagon and
   then we'll take it home.
Let them march around the room as they sing the song.

Dragon Day #3

Feature Focus Watch the film *Dragon Stew*.

Learning Labs

★ Make "Dragon Soup" with the class. Help the children peel and cut up ½ cup diced potatoes, 1 cup green peas, ½ cup sliced carrots, ¼ cup celery, 1 chopped tomato, and 2 tablespoons chopped onions. Place in a large pot with 4 cups of beef broth and bring to a boil. Lower heat, cover, and cook for 30 minutes. Add salt, pepper, and cooked meat if desired. Simmer another 10 minutes. Serve in small plastic cups for the children's snack. Makes twelve ½ cup servings.

★ Provide paint, paper, and brushes in the art area. Have children paint pictures of dragons making stew.

Think and Talk Time

★ Watch the film with the class. Discuss the unusual dishes that are mentioned in the film. Pretend to be a king who wants a new cook. Have the children pretend to be villagers who want to be the king's cook. Ask each child to suggest an unusual dish to the king.

★ Discuss how the king's new cook managed to make dishes exactly the way the king liked them. Did the dragon stew actually contain dragon meat?

Project Pursuits

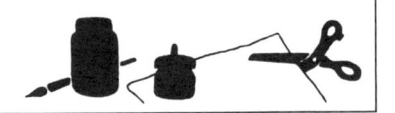

★ Have the class create a "Dragon Cookbook." Ask each child to dictate a recipe for such exotic dishes as "Dragon Eggs," "Dragon Cake," or "Dragon Sandwiches." Let children choose their own "recipes" and ingredients. You should record the information and procedure verbatim. Ask a volunteer to type up the recipes. Encourage each child to illustrate his or her recipe with crayon drawings or magazine collages.

★ Make a "Dragon Movie" with the class. Divide the class into small groups. Tell each group to make up stories and pictures about a dragon who likes to cook. When they have illustrated the pictures, tape the pictures together in a long line and roll them up onto paper towel rolls. Attach the roll to a box for stability. Let the children tell about their dragons as you unwind the drawings from the roll, one-by-one.

Movement Models

★ Play a game called "Catch the Dragon." Mark off a goal line and have the students stand on the line. Choose one child to be the dragon and have this child stand some distance away from the line, with his or her back towards the other children. The children chant, "Dragon, dragon, we're going to catch you. We'll take you home and turn you into stew." While they chant, the children creep closer to the dragon. At some point, the dragon claps his or her hands as a signal for the other children to run back to the line. Any child that is tagged by the dragon helps the dragon tag the rest of the children.

★ Choose one child to be a dragon. Ask the rest of the children to hold hands, forming a circle to represent a dragon cage. Teach the children to say, "One, two, three, four, I caught a dragon by the door. Five, six, seven, eight, I let it go outside the gate." On the word "eight," the children hold up their hands, forming arches. The dragon tries to escape before the children put their arms down again on the words "the gate."

Elephant Days

Pattern Page

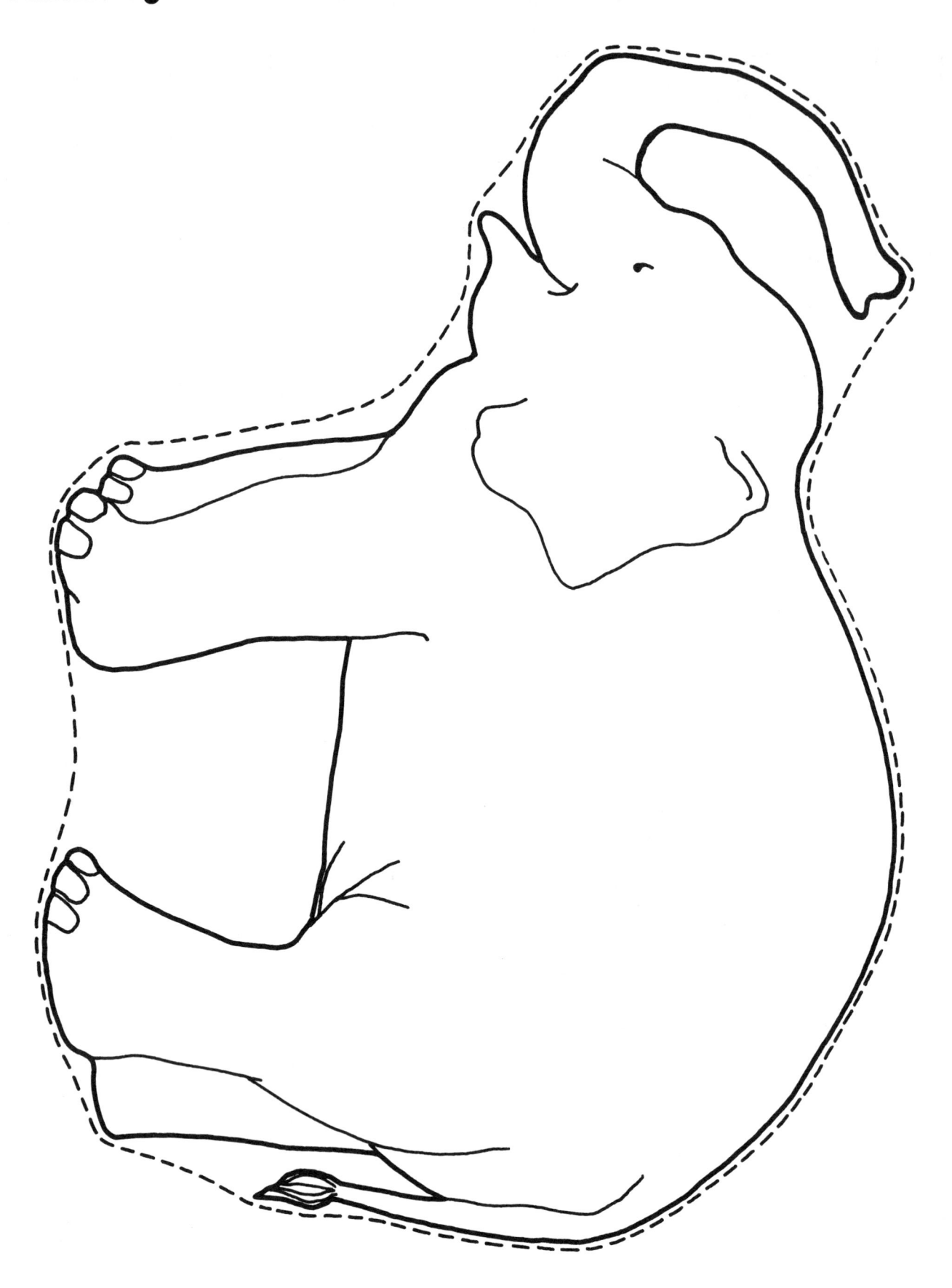

44

Elephant Days

Timing
>When the circus comes to town
>Before visiting a zoo

What Children Bring
>An elephant. (This can be a stuffed animal, a plastic animal, a picture, or a statue.)

Previous Day Reminder
>A gray construction-paper elephant ear pinned to each child's clothing.

Ready Resources

Books
>Dr. Seuss. *Horton Hatches an Egg.* New York: Random House, 1940.
>Griffin, Russel M. *The Blind Men and the Elephant.* New York: Timescape, 1982.
>Hamsa, Bobbie. *Your Pet Elephant.* Chicago: Childrens Press, 1980. (See related activities, page 47.)
>Hoffman, Mary. *Animals in the Wild: Elephants.* New York: Random House, 1984.
>Kipling, Rudyard. *The Elephant's Child.* Englewood Cliffs, NJ: Prentice-Hall, 1987. (See related activities, page 48.)
>Lobel, Arnold. *Uncle Elephant.* New York: Harper & Row, 1986.
>Mayer, Mercer. *Ah-Choo.* New York: Dial Books, 1976.
>Murphy, Jill. *Five Minutes' Peace.* New York: Putnam, 1986.
>Peet, Bill. *The Ant and the Elephant.* Boston: Houghton Mifflin, 1972.
>———. *Encore for Eleanor.* Boston: Houghton Mifflin, 1985.
>Vipont, Elfrida. *The Elephant and the Bad Baby.* New York: Putnam, 1986.

Films
>Steven Bosustow Productions. *How the Elephant Got His Trunk.* Deerfield, IL: Learning Corporation of America, 1970. (See related activities, page 48.)

Poems
>Anonymous. "Elephant Carries a Great Big Trunk." In *Read-Aloud Rhymes for the Very Young.* Jack Prelutsky, ed. New York: Knopf, 1984.
>Link, Lenore M. "Holding Hands." In *Read-Aloud Rhymes for the Very Young.* Jack Prelutsky, ed. New York: Knopf, 1984.
>Richards, Laura E. "Eletelephony." In *Piping Down the Valleys Wild.* Nancy Larrick, ed. New York: Delacorte Press, 1985.

Records and Songs
>Palmer, Hap. "The Elephant." On *Learning Basic Skills Through Music,* Vol 1. Educational Activities. (AR) 514. (See related activities, page 46.)
>Raffi. "Willoughby, Wallaby, Woo." On *Singable Songs for the Very Young.* Shoreline Records. (SLN) 0202.

Elephant Day #1

Feature Focus Read the book *The Blind Men and the Elephant*. Listen to the song "The Elephant."

Learning Labs

★ Have children work in teams of two to make elephants out of boxes, spools, and other "junk" items. Ask them to dictate a few words about their finished projects.

★ Cut out different sizes of elephants from gray construction paper. Leave in a learning area. Have students sort or sequence by size.

Think and Talk Time

★ Show the class a picture of an elephant. Ask the students to describe the animal. What are its ears like? What are its legs like? What is its tail like? What does its skin look like? After the discussion, read the book to the children. Ask them to think of other things that are like an elephant's ear, tail, side, legs, and trunk.

★ Have the children share the elephants they brought from home. If possible, ask each child to point out the ears, legs, trunks, body, and tail on his or her elephant.

Project Pursuits

★ Have the children construct "Stand-Up Elephants." Have each child fold a 6" × 9" piece of colored construction paper in half. Show the children how to cut a "hill" on the unfolded side of the paper to form legs.

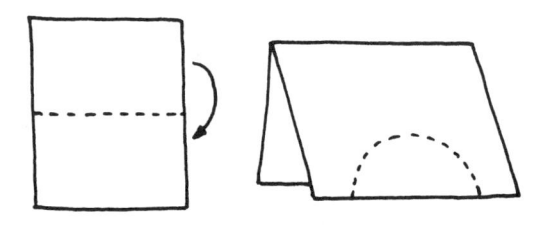

★ Have the students cut out two ovals from another 6" × 9" piece of paper in a contrasting color. Glue one oval on for a head. Cut the other oval in half and glue each piece on one side of the head for ears. Add a strip of ½" × 3" paper that has been curled around a pencil for a trunk. Use stick-on dots or markers to add eyes and features. Glue a small piece of string or yarn to the elephant for a tail.

Movement Models

★ Have children do an "Elephant Walk." Show them how to form an elephant trunk by holding their arms down in front of them and clasping their hands together. Play the song and ask them to pretend that they are very large elephants. Have the students swing their "trunks" as they move around the play area.

★ Play a version of "Who is the Leader?" Ask the children to stand in a circle. Ask one child to go out of the room. Choose another child to be the lead elephant. Ask all the children to bend over and form trunks with their hands. The lead elephant leads the group in performing a number of "trunk" motions, such as swinging trunks, shaking trunks, waving trunks, and circling trunks. When the child from outside comes back in, he or she must decide who the lead elephant is.

Elephant Day #2

Feature Focus Read the book *Your Pet Elephant*.

Learning Labs

★ Write simple math problems on gray elephant cutouts. Write the corresponding answers on brown paper peanuts. Place the elephants and the peanuts in a learning area. Have the children match each peanut with the appropriate elephant.

★ Provide the children with gray paint, paper, and brushes in an art area. Let each child paint a picture of an elephant. Provide photos as models.

Think and Talk Time

★ Have the children share the elephants they brought from home. Ask the children what would happen if the elephants they brought suddenly became alive. What would these mini-elephants be like? How would their lives be different from full-sized elephants?

★ Have the children pretend that they have the opportunity to get a baby elephant as a pet. How would they convince their parents that an elephant would make a good pet? What are some reasons that their parents might give for not wanting an elephant around the house? Keep a list of the children's suggestions.

★ Read the book to the class. Why does the author think an elephant would make a good pet? Why does the author think an elephant would make a bad pet? Compare the reasons in the book with the children's list of reasons.

Project Pursuits

★ Have the children illustrate a scene that shows what it would be like to have a pet elephant. Encourage the children to include themselves in the pictures. Have them add in features and background with markers or crayons. After the pictures are finished, have each child write or dictate a few sentences about the picture. Display on a classroom wall or bulletin board.

★ Use peanuts in the shell to create math problems for the class. Pass out peanuts to each child. Then tell the class a story. For example, you might say, "Your pet elephant had six peanuts." (Have the children count out six peanuts.) "Then the elephant ate two peanuts." (Have the children shell and eat two peanuts.) "How many peanuts does your elephant have left?" Continue using other addition and subtraction problems.

Movement Models

★ Play a game called "My Pet Elephant Says." Tell the children to stand like elephants—bent over with arms clasped together like trunks. Explain that you will give them a direction. They should only perform the action if you precede your direction by saying, "My pet elephant says." Ask the children to make motions such as walking backwards, walking in a circle swinging their "trunks" to the left, waving their trunks up and down, and reaching their trunks high in the air.

★ Play "Feed the Elephant." Tape a large piece of paper to the floor. Draw four or five large elephant faces on it. In each elephant's trunk, write a numeral. Let the children take turns "feeding the elephants" by tossing "peanuts" (tan beanbags) onto the elephant faces. Tell the children to keep track of the points they get by counting out real peanuts. At the end of the game, ask all the children to count their peanuts.

Elephant Day #3

Feature Focus Watch the film "How the Elephant Got His Trunk" or read the book *The Elephant's Child.*

Learning Labs

★ Make "Elephant Trunks" for the children to use in a creative play area. Cut off the feet from old stockings, and tie the ends closed. Stuff each stocking leg with pillow stuffing. Sew to close and attach elastic so children can wear the trunks.

★ Let the children make elephants out of playdough.

Think and Talk Time

★ Brainstorm with the children to create a list of possibilities as to why elephants have trunks. How did the elephants get their trunks? After the discussion, read the story or watch the film. Ask the children if they think an elephant's nose could have really stretched that much. Why or why not? Discuss how the baby elephant's mother, father, and friends reacted to his new trunk.

★ Discuss the ways in which an elephant's trunk helps the elephant. Show the children pictures of elephants using their trunks to perform different actions. Ask the class to tell a story about a little elephant who does not have a long trunk. How does the elephant feed and wash itself? How does it pick up things?

Project Pursuits

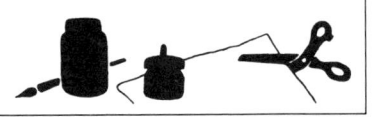

★ Have the class make a "Limpopo River Mural." Cover a wall with a large piece of butcher paper. Draw an outline of the Limpopo across the length of the paper. Have the children work in pairs along sections of the mural. Ask them to add construction paper details and animals along the banks of the Limpopo. After the mural is finished, you might have children take turns telling stories about traveling down the river in a boat.

★ Create a class book titled "How an Elephant Uses Its Trunk." Have each child draw a picture of an elephant using its trunk. Staple the final pictures inside a piece of folded gray construction paper and write the title on the cover.

★ Have the children make elephants with movable trunks. Have each child draw and cut out a large elephant head from construction paper. Then have each child cut out a trunk. With brass fasteners, connect the trunks to the elephants' faces. The children can move the trunk into different positions.

Movement Models

★ Play "Elephant Chain." Ask the children to form a line—each child with his or her hands on the waist of the next child in line. Tuck a gray scarf into the belt or waistband of the last child in line. The children in the line are elephants. The first person in line tries to grab the last elephant's tail (the scarf) by maneuvering the line around. After the tail is pulled off, the first child in line goes to the end of the line and puts on the elephant's tail. Continue playing until all the children have had a chance to wear the tail and be the leader.

★ Have the children play "Elephant Soccer." Ask the children to form a circle, each child standing with feet wide apart. Ask the children to hold their arms down in front of them like trunks. Have them use only their trunks to roll a ball across the circle trying to get it through someone's legs. If the ball does go out, the person whose legs it rolled through must retrieve the ball.

Foot Days

Pattern Page

50

Foot Days

Timing
> During a health unit
> During a science unit
> May (Official Foot Health Month)

Morning Preview
> Before class, place cutout footprints in the hall leading into the classroom. Place more prints around the room. Have children follow the prints as they walk in.

Ready Resources

Books

Bailey, Jill. *Feet.* New York: Putnam, 1984. (See related activities, page 53.)
De Regniers, Beatrice S. *What Can You Do with a Shoe?* New York: Harper & Row, 1955.
Dr. Seuss. *The Foot Book.* New York: Random House, 1968. (See related activities, page 52.)
Goor, Ron, and Nancy Goor. *All Kinds of Feet.* New York: Crowell, 1984. (See related activities, page 53.)
Kroll, Steven. *Dirty Feet.* New York: Parents Magazine Press, 1981.
Myller, Rolf. *How Big Is a Foot?* New York: Atheneum, 1979.
Rice, Eve. *New Blue Shoes.* New York: Viking-Penguin, 1979.
Watson, Elizabeth. *Busy Feet.* Cincinnati, OH: Standard Publishing, 1981.
Winthrop, Elizabeth. *Shoes.* New York: Harper & Row, 1986. (See related activites, page 54.)

Films

Magic Sneakers. Chicago: Encyclopedia Britannica Educational Corporation, 1969. (See related activities, page 54.)

Poems

Hillert, Margaret. "About Feet." In *Random House Book of Poetry for Children.* Jack Prelutsky, ed. New York: Random House, 1983.
Merriam, Eve. "Left Foot, Right Foot." In *Blackberry Ink.* New York: Morrow, 1985.

Records and Songs

Glazer, Tom. "Shoemaker, Shoemaker." In *Eye Winker, Tom Tinker, Chin Chopper.* New York: Doubleday, 1973.
Hallum, Rosemary, and Henry Glass. "Footplay." On *Fingerplays and Footplays.* Educational Activities. (AR) 618.
Mitchell, Don. "Feet, Feet, Feet." On *All Aboard the Good Apple Music Train.* Good Apple. (GA) 123. (See related activities, page 52.)

Foot Day #1

Feature Focus Read the book *The Foot Book*.
Listen to the song "Feet, Feet, Feet."

Learning Labs

★ Let the children use "Foot Rulers" to measure objects around the room. Cut out a 12" foot shape from cardboard. Mark off inches down a line in the middle of the foot.

★ Make a special "Foot Feeling" area in the classroom. Put different textures of materials on the floor, such as cardboard, smooth wood, fake grass, and shag rugs. Have children take off their shoes and explore the different textures with their bare feet.

★ Let the children make "Foot People." Have each child trace around his or her foot or shoe and cut out. This piece is the body. Ask the children to add arms, legs, and facial features using pieces of scrap paper. Let children add details with other scrap materials.

Think and Talk Time

★ Ask the children to tell you different ways in which we use our feet. Encourage the children to go beyond the simple answers of walking and running. Read the book to the class. Discuss ways in which we can keep our feet healthy.

★ Introduce the foot as a unit of measure. Measure an object by walking heel-to-toe along the length of the object. Repeat with a child's foot and with the standard measure. Compare the differences. Then tell the story of how the foot came to be a standard unit of measure.

Project Pursuits

★ Have each child trace around his or her foot onto a piece of white construction paper. Have the child move the foot slightly and trace again. Repeat this several times—the foot outlines should overlap somewhat. Ask children to use bright colors of crayons or markers to fill in the overlapping areas.

★ Have the children make footprints on a large piece of brown butcher paper. Let the children put a foot into a shallow pan of paint and stamp the foot onto the paper. (Have plenty of newspaper around for the activity.) Hang the finished picture on a wall under the caption "Footprints in the Sand." Have students compare the footprints. Point out that each print is unique. Listen to the song during this activity.

Movement Models

★ Have the children explore all the movements of feet, such as walking, dancing, galloping, hopping, skipping, marching, jumping, kicking, and tiptoeing, in time to music. If possible, let the children do this activity outside. Find an area which is safe from broken glass or other dangerous materials. Let everyone take off their shoes and feel the ground as they move.

★ Have the children take off their shoes. Ask them to pretend they have strings tied to their big toes. Have them "pull" on the imaginary strings and let go. Ask them to try walking while they pretend to pull on the strings.

★ Have the children do other movements with their bare toes. For example, you might have them sit down and do "toe dances" in time to tap-dance music, or you might have them draw imaginary circles, squares, and other shapes in the air with their toes.

Foot Day #2

Feature Focus Read the books *Feet* and *All Kinds of Feet*.

Learning Labs

★ Leave pictures of animal faces and feet in a learning center. Have children match each foot picture to the correct animal face.

★ Make an interactive bulletin board. Cut out or draw pictures of animals with two feet and animals with four feet. Pin corresponding captions on the board. Have the children sort the pictures and pin them under the appropriate heading.

Think and Talk Time

★ Brainstorm with the children to create a list of animals that have no feet, two feet, four feet, and six feet. Point out that different animals have different types of feet. Ask the children to suggest reasons for this. Help them understand that the different types of feet help the different animals live in different types of places or situations.

★ Read and show the books to the children. Compare the animals mentioned in the books to those the children suggested. Were there any animals that the books mentioned that the children did not? Were there any animals that the children mentioned that the books did not?

★ Compare human feet to animal feet. How do our feet help us? Ask the children to pretend they have four legs. Let them crawl around the room on all fours. Ask them to tell you things that they cannot do while they are on all fours.

Project Pursuits

★ Have the children make "Animal Foot Collages." Divide the class into groups and have each group work on a collage that shows animals with no feet, with two feet, with four feet, or with six feet. Have the children cut out pictures of the appropriate animals from magazines. Let them glue the pictures onto a large piece of construction paper. Encourage the children to find as wide a range of animals as possible.

★ Play "Animal Foot Bingo." Make bingo cards using drawings of different animal feet instead of numbers. Make five columns and five rows on each card. Call out an animal and have the children cover that particular animal foot if it appears on their cards. If you wish, before playing, make up a master chart that shows the different animals and their feet. The first child with five spaces covered in a row calls out "Animal Feet!" This child becomes the next leader.

Movement Models

★ Ask children to pretend they are different animals. Have them move around like animals that have different numbers and types of feet. For example, you might have them pretend to be snakes slithering across the floor; ducks waddling around the play area; bears lumbering on all fours. For eight-legged spiders, have each child choose a partner and get down on hands and knees with the partner to form an eight-legged animal. Ask the children to try to stay together as they crawl forward and backward.

★ Play "Animal Track Relay." Divide the class into four groups and call each group by an animal name, such as bears, rabbits, deer, and birds. Copy and cut out animals' tracks that correspond to the animal groups. Arrange the tracks in random patterns on the floor. One child from each group has to follow the tracks of his or her animal to a goal line and back again. When the child returns, he or she tags the next child in line who repeats the same procedure.

Foot Day #3

Feature Focus Watch the film *Magic Sneakers*. Read the book *Shoes*.

Learning Labs

★ Put men's and women's shoes in the dress-up area. Let children use and wear the shoes during playtime.

★ Cut out or draw pictures of pairs of shoes. Put each shoe picture on a separate card. Ask the children to find the matching left and right shoes.

Think and Talk Time

★ Show the children several shoes from the dress-up area. Describe one of the shoes and ask children to identify the shoe you are describing. Display more shoes, and give children a chance to "describe" shoes to the rest of the class. Show the children pictures from the book. Ask them how they would describe some of the shoes that are pictured.

★ Brainstorm with the class to create a list of shoe names; for example, sneakers, slippers, and boots. Point out that different people wear different shoes. Who are some people who wear special shoes on their jobs? What types of shoes do they wear? Why? Read the book.

★ Show the class a sneaker. Ask the children to pretend that this sneaker is magic. Have the children suggest things they would be able to do if they wore magic sneakers. After the discussion, show the film.

Project Pursuits

★ Have the children make "Shoe Scrapbooks." Let the children cut out pictures from catalogs and magazines and glue them onto pieces of paper. Have the children draw in the people wearing the shoes and backgrounds showing what the people are doing. Show the children how to punch holes through the book and tie the pages together with yarn. If possible, help the children name the different types of shoes in their books.

★ Encourage students to draw pictures of themselves wearing magic sneakers. Have each child draw a picture that shows himself or herself doing something he or she might not be able to do normally. Have the children write or dictate a story about the picture and the sneakers.

Movement Models

★ Play "Sock Ball Toss" with the children. Divide the class into groups of three or four. Give each group several rolled-up socks and a pair of large shoes. Place the heels of the shoes up on blocks and have the children try to throw the socks into the shoes. Keep track of individual scores by making a tally mark each time a sock is thrown into a shoe.

★ Have the children take off their shoes and put the shoes on their hands. Ask them to "walk" the shoes in different ways, such as walking forward, walking backward, walking in the air, and walking one shoe to each side.

★ Play a game called "Pass the Shoes." Have the children sit in a circle. Ask the children to pass shoes around the circle at the same time in time to music. (Note—any music with a definite beat will work for this activity.)

Frog Days

Pattern Page

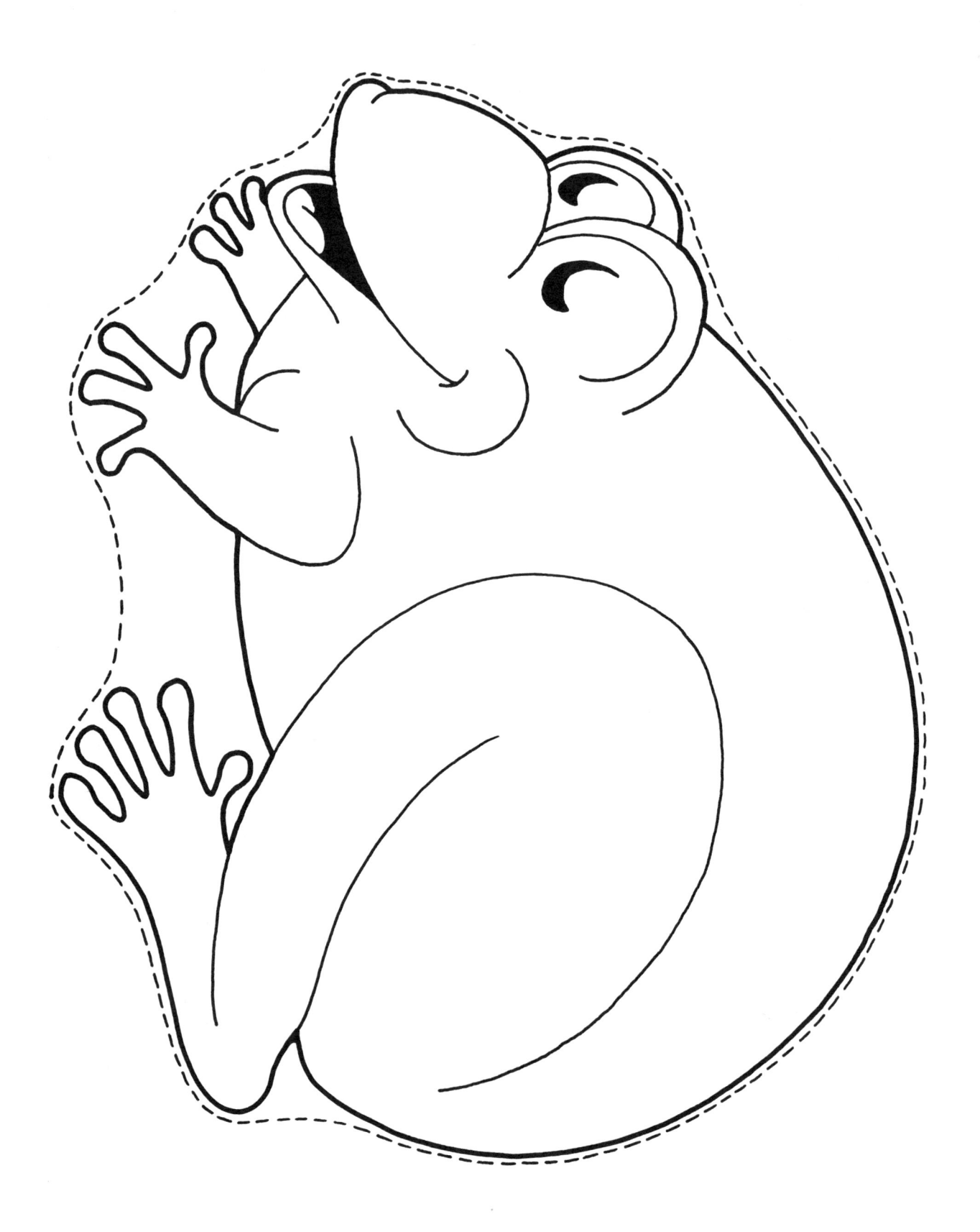

Frog Days

Timing
   Spring
   During a nature unit
   During an alphabet unit

What Children Bring
   A frog. (This can be a stuffed animal, a plastic animal, a picture, or a statue.)

Previous Day Reminder
   A green stick-on dot on each child's hand.

Ready Resources

Books
   Cole, Joanna. *A Frog's Body*. New York: Morrow, 1980. (See related activities, page 58.)
   Langstaff, John, and Feodor Rojankosky. *Frog Went A-Courtin'*. San Diego, CA: Harcourt Brace Jovanovich, 1972. (See related activities, page 60.)
   Lane, Margaret. *The Frog*. New York: Dial Books, 1981. (See related activities, page 58.)
   Lobel, Arnold. *Frog and Toad Are Friends*. New York: Harper & Row, 1979. (See related activities, page 59.)
   _____. *Frog and Toad Together*. New York: Harper & Row, 1979. (See related activities, page 59.)
   Mayer, Mercer. *A Boy, a Dog, and a Frog*. New York: Dial Books, 1979.
   _____. *One Frog Too Many*. New York: Dial Books, 1975.

Films
   Frog Went A-Courtin'. Weston, CT: Weston Woods Studios, 1955. (See related activities, page 60.)

Poems
   Aiken, Conrad. "Frog." In *An Arkful of Animals*. William Cole, ed. Boston: Houghton Mifflin, 1978.
   Guiterman, Arthur. "The Polliwog." In *Random House Book of Poetry for Children*. Jack Prelutsky, ed. New York: Random House, 1983.
   Luton, Mildred. "Bullfrog Communique." In *An Arkful of Animals*. William Cole, ed. Boston: Houghton Mifflin, 1978.
   Moore, John T. "The Tree Frog." In *Random House Book of Poetry for Children*. Jack Prelutsky, ed. New York: Random House, 1983.

Records and Songs
   Ives, Burl. "Mr. Froggie Went A-Courtin'." On *Burl Ives Sings Little White Duck and Other Songs*. Columbia. (PC) 33183. (See related activities, page 60.)
   Palmer, Hap. "Jumping Frog." On *Pretend*. Educational Activities. (AR) 563. (See related activities, page 58.)

Frog Day #1

Feature Focus Read the book *A Frog's Body* or *The Frog*. Listen to the song "Jumping Frog."

Learning Labs

★ If possible, bring in live frogs for the children to examine.

★ Make "Frog Puzzles" for the children. Glue photographs of frogs that have been cut out of magazines onto pieces of tagboard. Cut the pictures into puzzle pieces. Leave in a learning area for the children to put together.

Think and Talk Time

★ Discuss frogs—what they are, what they look like, where they live, and what they eat. Use one or both of the books to illustrate the discussion. Ask children to share the frogs they brought from home, pointing out different parts on the body.

★ Help children understand the life cycle of a frog. Use simple drawings on a flannel board to illustrate the sequence of changes in the life of a frog. After the discussion, let the children sequence the pictures while they name each stage.

Project Pursuits

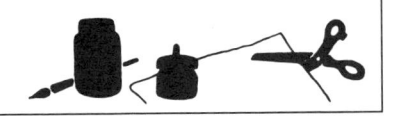

★ Have the children make a "Frog in a Pond" diorama. Supply children with small plastic frogs or have them make their own frogs out of green playdough. Also give each child a shoe box top, a piece of blue paper, a few small stones, and some dried weeds or grasses. Have each child cut out a pond shape from the blue paper and glue it into the shoe box top. Then have them arrange the rocks, grasses, bits of playdough, and frogs in the tops. Glue down each piece after the children are satisfied with the arrangements. Have each child write or dictate a few sentences about frogs to be displayed with the diorama.

★ Give each child a frog sticker or a cutout paper frog to incorporate into a picture. Ask the children to illustrate something about frog life. Have the children dictate or write a few remarks about what the frogs are doing in their pictures. Display on a wall or a bulletin board under the caption, "It's a Frog's Life."

Movement Models

★ Teach the children how to do frog jumps. Have them squat down in a crouched position, then spring up with a jump. Let them practice different types of jumps—short jumps, long jumps, fast jumps, and slow jumps. Play the song and have the children jump around the room, pretending to be in a large swamp. You might lay out carpet square "lily pads" for the children to rest on.

★ Have the children run "Frog Jump Relays." Divide the class into two teams. Clearly mark off a starting line and turn-around line. Ask the teams to line up behind the starting line. Then have the first child in each line "frog jump" to the turn-around line and back again. When the child returns, he or she tags the next child in line who repeats the procedure. To make this more difficult, place several tires in the path to the turn-around line. Ask children to jump in and out of each tire.

Frog Day #2

Feature Focus Read the book *Frog and Toad Are Friends* or *Frog and Toad Together*.

Learning Labs

★ Cut out frog shapes from green paper and toad shapes from brown paper. On each frog write a lower-case letter. Write the corresponding capital letters on each toad. Have children match the corresponding frogs and toads.

★ Leave green and brown paint in the art area. Have children paint pictures of frogs and toads. Display photographs for inspiration.

Think and Talk Time

★ Have the children share the frogs they brought from home. Ask each child to tell three facts about his or her frog.

★ Show the book to the children. Have the class tell the story as they view the pictures. Discuss the characters of Frog and Toad. How are they alike? How are they different? What is special about their friendship?

★ Have children discuss special friendships that they have had. What makes these friendships special?

★ Discuss the differences between frogs and toads. If possible, obtain pictures of the different animals for the children to compare. Point out that toads tend to spend less time in the water; are generally shorter and squatter; have weaker hind legs; and have rough, dry, and warty skin rather than smooth and moist skin.

Project Pursuits

★ Create a class book titled "Frog and Toad Are Together Again." Have each child draw a picture of Frog and Toad doing something together. If you wish, ask the children to dictate or write a few sentences about the pictures. Place the finished drawings together inside a piece of folded construction paper. Write the title on the cover.

★ Let the children make frog and toad puppets. Give each child two small paper plates. Ask the children to paint one plate green and the other plate brown. Have them add construction-paper mouths, legs, and eyes to the plates. Attach each plate to a tongue depressor or a straw. Let the children use their puppets to put on shows about the friendship of Frog and Toad.

Movement Models

★ Play a game called "Frogs and Toads." Divide the class into two teams. Call one team the frogs and the other the toads. Have the teams stand on opposite goal lines facing each other. Ask the frogs to turn their backs, then have the toads quietly "hop" up to the frogs. When you call out, "The toads are coming!" the frogs turn around and chase the toads back to their goal line. Tagged players become part of the frog team. Play the game again, having the frogs "hop" up to the toads.

★ Play "Frog and Toad Together." Direct the children to find partners. One child in each pair is Frog and the other is Toad. The partners stand facing each other. Call out a body part command, such as "Frog and Toad, nose to nose." Call out as many different body parts as you can, using the terms *left* and *right* in your directions. Occasionally have the children switch partners.

Frog Day #3

Feature Focus Read the book or watch the film *Frog Went A-Courtin'*. Listen to the song "Mr. Froggie Went A-Courtin'."

Learning Labs

★ Draw or cut out pictures of the different animals in the book, such as frog, mouse, and rat. Also draw or cut out pictures of objects that rhyme with the characters names, such as a log, a house, and a hat. Glue each picture onto a separate index card. Leave in a learning center. Have the children match each character picture with the correct rhyming word picture.

★ Collect plastic frogs or make paper frogs. Write numerals or simple addition problems on separate index cards. Have the students draw a card and place the corresponding number of frogs on a green felt lily pad.

★ Let the children make frogs out of green playdough.

Think and Talk Time

★ Read the book or watch the film. Have the children make up new verses for the story. You might ask them to talk about what happens after Frog and Mouse get married. Let the students retell the story using a flannel board and cutout felt characters.

★ Point out the rhyming words in the story. Brainstorm with the children to create a list of words that rhyme with frog.

Project Pursuits

★ Divide the class into groups of three or four. Have each group construct a room for Frog's and Mouse's new house. Let the children make furniture and decorations out of boxes, spools, fabric, and other materials from a scrap box. Ask them to place the objects inside a shoe box that has been turned on its side. After the children have finished, have them dictate or write a few sentences about their dioramas. Display on a classroom table or desk.

★ Create a classroom book titled, "If I Were a Frog." Have each child glue a picture of his or her face to a piece of paper. Ask the children to draw a frog's body around the face. Have them add in details and backgrounds that show things that they would do if they were frogs. Have the children complete the following sentence: "If I were a frog I would _____." The sentences should be written at the bottom of the picture. Place inside folded construction paper and write the title on the cover.

Movement Models

★ Play the song and have the children pantomime the actions of the characters. If you wish, assign each child to be a particular character. Have the children act out only their parts during the song.

★ Play "Frog on a Log." Mark out a circle on the floor. Choose one child to be Froggie. Froggie sits in the middle of the circle. The other children are mice. The mice creep toward the center of the circle, chanting "Frog, Frog, get off of your log." Froggie tries to tag any mouse that comes near him or her. If a child is tagged, he or she sits down next to Froggie and helps him or her tag the rest of the mice. Play until six or seven children have been tagged.

Giant Days

Pattern Page

62

Giant Days

Timing
   Anytime

Previous Day Preview
   Just before the children leave, ask them to think about what it would be like if they grew eight feet overnight.

Ready Resources

Books
   Balian, Lorna. *A Sweetheart for Valentine*. Nashville, TN: Abingdon, 1979.
   Briggs, Raymond. *Jim and the Beanstalk*. New York: Putnam, 1970. (See related activities, page 65.)
   De Paola, Tomie. *Fin M'Coul*. New York: Holiday House, 1981.
   _____. *The Mysterious Giant at Barletta*. San Diego, CA: Harcourt Brace Jovanovich, 1984.
   De Regniers, Beatrice S. *Jack the Giant Killer*. New York: Atheneum, 1987.
   Galdone, Paul. *Jack and the Beanstalk*. Boston: Houghton Mifflin, 1982. (See related activities, page 65.)
   Harrison, D.L. *The Book of Giant Stories*. New York: McGraw-Hill, 1972.
   Kellogg, Steven. *Much Bigger Than Martin*. New York: Dial Books, 1976. (See related activities, page 66.)
   Kroll, Steven. *Giant's Journey*. New York: Holiday House, 1981.
   Lobel, Arnold. *Giant John*. New York: Harper & Row, 1964.
   _____. *Prince Bertram, The Bad*. New York: Harper & Row, 1963.
   Sherman, Ivan. *I Am a Giant*. San Diego, CA: Harcourt Brace Jovanovich, 1975. (See related activities, page 64.)

Poems
   Silverstein, Shel. "Me and My Giant." In *Where the Sidewalk Ends*. New York: Harper & Row, 1974. (See related activities, page 64.)

Records and Songs
   Palmer, Hap. "The Friendly Giant" On *Pretend*. Educational Activities. (AR) 563. (See related activities, page 64.)

Short Stories
   O'Brien, Edna. "Two Giants." In *Tales for the Telling*. Jonathan Lanman. New York: Macmillan, 1986.

Teacher Resources
   Dunn, Lloyd M., et. al. *Peabody Language Development Kit, Level 1*. Poster 5. Circle Pines, MN: American Guidance Service, 1981.

Giant Day #1

Feature Focus   Read the book *I Am a Giant* and the poem "Me and My Giant." Listen to the song "Friendly Giant."

Learning Labs

★ Set up a small village in a creative play area so children can feel like giants as they play. Draw streets and roads on a large piece of cloth. Add small toy buildings, cars, and people. (Fisher-Price has several play sets that contain durable pieces perfect for this type of role-playing.)

★ Replace all the regular-size paper, brushes, and paint jars in the art area with small pieces of paper, tiny brushes, and paint in milk-jug lids. Encourage students to paint pictures, using this equipment, that show what it is like to be a giant.

Think and Talk Time

★ Discuss giants with the class. What would the children do if they suddenly turned into giants? Brainstorm with the children to create a list of objects giants could use if they wanted to take baths, blow their noses, or drink milk. Read the book.

★ Read the poem. Discuss what the children would do if a friendly giant came to visit. What would they feed the giant? Where would the giant sleep? What games could they play with the giant?

Project Pursuits

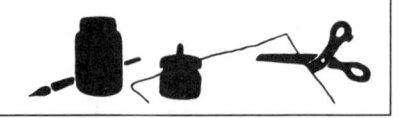

★ Have the children make tiny "Clothespin People." Ask the children to pretend they are giants while they work on the project. Give each child one or two wood clothespins. Show them how to make the clothespins into people by decorating the clothespins with paper, glue, markers, and yarn. Have the children put on a show with the people they make.

★ On extra-large paper, draw a picture of a giant. Let each child add a photo of himself or herself to the picture. Ask the children to add a background and dictate a story about playing with the giant. Write the story at the bottom of the picture.

Movement Models

★ Spread the pieces from the *Learning Labs* village around the room. Play the instrumental side of the record and have the children march around the room pretending to be friendly giants. Repeat the activity using the vocal side of the album. Ask children to sing the song as they march.

★ Play a game called "Giant in a Cave." Have the students stand on a goal line. Choose one child to be the giant. Have the giant stand some distance from the base and turn his or her back on the other children. The students start to creep toward the giant as the giant chants, "Fee, Fie, Foe, Fum, I'll catch you if you don't run." On the word *run*, the students start to run back to the goal line while the giant tries to tag them. Any child who is tagged helps the giant tag the other children. When all the untagged children have reached the goal line, the giant and the tagged children turn their backs and chant the lines again. Continue playing until three-fourths of the students have been tagged.

Giant Day #2

Feature Focus Read the books *Jack and the Beanstalk* and *Jim and the Beanstalk*.

Learning Labs

★ Help the children plant bean seeds in paper cups. Let the children water the seeds. Have students examine the seeds for growth. Do they grow like the bean seeds that Jack got?

★ Create a "Giant's House" drama area by placing grown-up clothes and large furniture in a creative play area.

Think and Talk Time

★ Read both books to the children—*Jack* first and then *Jim*. Ask the children to compare the two books. How had the giant changed over time? How were Jack and Jim alike? How were they different?

★ Point out that Jack takes things from the giant, while Jim brings things to the giant. Brainstorm with the children to create a list of things they could do to help the giant. Ask the children to describe what it would be like to help the giant.

Project Pursuits

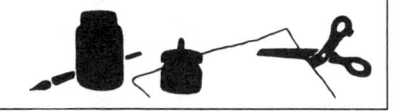

★ Make a class bulletin board captioned "Kids and the Beanstalk." Make a beanstalk on the board using green yarn and construction-paper leaves. Have each child add pictures of himself or herself climbing the beanstalk. If you wish, the faces of the children's pictures could be photographs of their faces. Add a cutout foot at the top of the beanstalk to show the giant. Pin the caption below the board.

★ Have each child write or dictate two short notes to the giant. They should pretend one note is from Jack and the other note is from Jim. Let them illustrate their notes with crayons or markers. Display the final projects on a classroom wall.

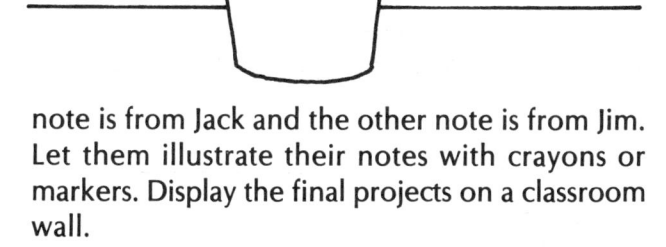

★ Have children use giant-size crayons to draw pictures that illustrate what it would be like to meet the giant. Encourage the children to include themselves in the pictures.

Movement Models

★ Have the children act out one of the stories. Divide the class into small groups so everyone gets a chance to play either the mother, the giant, Jack, or Jim.

★ Let the children pretend to climb up and down beanstalks in time to music. Show them how to do the hand-over-hand motion of someone climbing a rope.

★ Play a game called "Jack and Jim." Choose one child to be the giant. This person should stand on a line marked with tape or chalk. Have the other children stand in a row opposite the giant, some distance away. The giant stands with his or her back to the group and calls out "Jim" or "Jack." If the giant calls out "Jim," the students take giant steps toward the marked line. If the giant calls out "Jack," the children must take small backward steps. The game continues until one of the children reaches the marked line. That child becomes the new giant.

65

Giant Day #3

Feature Focus   Read the book *Much Bigger Than Martin*.

Learning Labs

★ Draw or cut out a series of pictures that shows a child changing and growing bigger. Place each picture on a piece of tagboard. Leave in a learning area for children to sequence.

★ Leave large pieces of paper in the art area. Let children use giant crayons to draw pictures of giants.

Think and Talk Time

★ Discuss what it would be like to be a giant with the class. Ask the children to suggest things that they would like and dislike about being a giant. Then brainstorm with the class to think of a list of things that would help the children grow into giants. Let the children use their imaginations.

★ Read the book to the children. Why did the little brother want to be a giant? How did he try to solve his problem? Why didn't his solution work? Point out that the little brother really just wanted to be bigger. Discuss things that the students might do when they are bigger that they can't do now. Record their answers. Then ask them to suggest some things that they can do now that they might not be able to do when they are older.

Project Pursuits

★ Have the children make a class book, with each child contributing a page. Ask the students to draw a picture on a piece of paper that shows something they would like to do when they are bigger. Have them complete the sentence, "When I'm much bigger, I want to _____."

On the other side of the paper, they should draw a picture of something they can do now. Ask them to complete the sentence, "However, since I'm small I can _____." Place the completed pages inside a piece of folded construction paper. Write the title, "Big and Small," on the cover.

★ Have the children draw a three-panel illustration. Give each child three pieces of paper taped together in a row. Ask the children to draw something big on the left-hand piece of paper, something bigger on the center piece of paper, and something much bigger on the right-hand piece of paper. Display the final drawings on a classroom wall.

Movement Models

★ Have the children pretend to grow "much bigger." Ask the children to crouch down on their knees. Then have them slowly rise to a standing position, finally standing on the tips of their toes, arms stretched above them.

★ Have a "Smaller, Bigger Relay Race." Divide the class into teams and mark off two goal lines. Explain that you are going to play some music. While the music is playing, the children may take giant steps toward the opposite goal line. When the music is turned off, the children must take teeny-tiny steps toward the goal line. Each child must reach the goal line, turn around, and get back to the opposite goal line to tag the next player. Turn the music on and off often.

Hat Days

Pattern Page

Hat Days

Timing
    Before Easter
    Hat Day (1/18)

What Children Bring
    A hat or a cap.

Previous Day Reminder
    A construction-paper hat pinned to each child's shirt.

Ready Resources

Books
    Berenstain, Stan, and Jan Berenstain. *Old Hat, New Hat*. New York: Random House, 1970.
    Blos, Joan W. *Martin's Hats*. New York: Mulberry Books, 1984. (See related activities, page 70.)
    Dr. Seuss. *The Five Hundred Hats of Bartholomew Cubbins*. New York: Vanguard Press, 1938.
    Duvoisin, Roger. *Jasmine*. New York: Knopf, 1973.
    Keats, Ezra J. *Jennie's Hat*. New York: Harper & Row, 1966.
    Kuskin, Karla. *The Boy Had a Mother Who Bought Him a Hat*. Boston: Houghton Mifflin, 1976.
    Lloyd, David. *Hat*. New York: Random House, 1984.
    Nodset, Joan L. *Who Took the Farmer's Hat?* New York: Harper & Row, 1963.
    Shortall, Leonard. *The Hat Book*. Racine, WI: Western, 1976.
    Slobodkina, Esphyr. *Caps for Sale*. New York: Scholastic, 1976. (See related activities, page 71.)
    Tomkins, Jasper. *The Catalog*. La Jolla, CA: Green Tiger Press, 1981.
    Ungerer, Tomi. *The Hat*. New York: Scholastic, 1982. (See related activities, page 72.)

Films
    Caps for Sale. Weston, CT: Weston Woods Studios. (See related activities, page 71.)
    De Noia, Nick. *Magic Hat*. Del Mar, CA: McGraw-Hill Films, 1980.

Records and Songs
    Beal, Pamela C., and Susan H. Nipp. "My Hat, It Has Three Corners." In *Wee Sing Silly Songs*. Los Angeles: Price, Stern, Sloan, 1983.
    Sharon, Lois, and Bram. "Tall Silk Hat." On *In the Schoolyard*. Elephant Records. (LFN) 8105.

Hat Day #1

Feature Focus   Read the book *Martin's Hats*.

Learning Labs

★ Place a variety of hats in a dress-up area. Let the children use the hats for spontaneous drama. Be sure to include hats from different occupations, such as firefighter hats, chef hats, nurse caps, and construction worker hats.

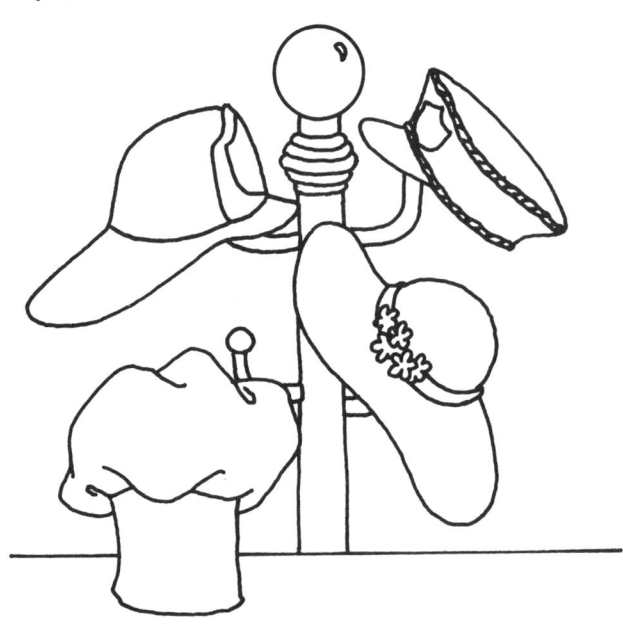

★ Obtain or draw pictures of people in different occupations and their hats. Glue each person and each hat on a separate piece of tagboard. Leave in a learning center. Have the students match each person with his or her hat.

★ Leave playdough in an art center. Let children make different hats out of the material.

Think and Talk Time

★ Brainstorm with the children to create a list of occupations in which people wear hats. Display and discuss hats that are associated with some of these jobs. Why is each hat suited to the particular occupation it is used in?

★ Read the book. Ask children to describe some of the things they would "become" if they had a large collection of hats like Martin. If each child could only have one of Martin's hats, which one would he or she want? Why?

Project Pursuits

★ Have the children create a classroom bulletin board. Have each child draw a picture of a hat he or she would like to wear. Ask each child to write or dictate a few lines about where he or she would wear the hat. Pin the pictures on a bulletin board under the caption "Classy Hats."

★ Have the children make "Hat Collages." Ask each child to draw an outline of a hat on a piece of paper. Then have the children glue scraps of fabric, foil, tissue paper, lace, or any other materials inside the outlines.

Movement Models

★ Play "Hat Charades" with the children. Draw or cut out pictures of different worker's hats. Glue each picture onto an index card. Place the cards in a box. Have the children sit in a circle. Choose one child to draw a card from the box. Have the child look at the picture and act out the job implied by the hat on the card. The rest of the children try to guess which worker the child is imitating. Whoever guesses correctly gets to choose the next card.

★ Play "Hat Toss." Choose several of the hats that the children brought from home. Place them top down on the floor. Supply the children with rolled-up pairs of socks. Have the children try to toss the socks into the hats. After a period of time, replace the hats with some others. Continue until all the hats have been used.

Hat Day #2

Feature Focus   Read the book or watch the film *Caps for Sale*.

Learning Labs

★ Cut identical hats out of different fabrics. Make several hats out of each fabric. Leave in a learning area. Have the children sort the hats into groups of matching fabrics.

★ Draw pictures of caps stacked on top of each other to represent the numerals 1–10. Have children sequence the pictures.

Think and Talk Time

★ Read the story or watch the film. Then retell the story using a flannel board. Cut the characters and caps out of felt and back with sandpaper. Have the students help you sort the different caps as you place them on the peddler's head.

★ Use paper caps to create "Stacked Caps" math problems. For example, place two paper caps on a table and say, "The peddler has two caps." Then place two more caps above these and say, "Here are two more caps." Ask the children to tell you how many caps there are all together. Then take away a cap, saying, "The monkey stole a cap. How many are left?"

Project Pursuits

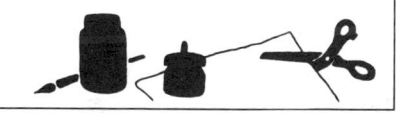

★ Have the children make their own flannel-board figures for mini-flannel boards. Have each child glue a piece of light blue felt on top of a shoe box. Have the children make a tree, the peddler, some monkeys, and several caps out of construction paper. Let them glue small pieces of sandpaper to the back of each piece. Retell the story and have the children manipulate their figures on the box top. The figures may be stored inside the box.

★ Let the children make caps for the peddler to sell. Have each child draw and color a cap on construction paper. Let them decorate the caps with feathers, fabric, lace, or other objects from a scrap box. Display the caps on a bulletin board under the caption, "Caps for Sale." You might have the children put price tags on their caps.

Movement Models

★ Use the hats that the children brought from home to pantomime the story. Let all the children have a chance to play a monkey or the peddler.

★ Play a game called "The Monkey and the Peddler." Have the children sit in a circle with hats on their heads. Choose one child to go around the circle. This child walks around the circle and taps each child, saying, "Peddler." At some point the child taps someone, says, "Monkey," and takes the child's hat. The child without a hat chases the first child around the circle trying to tag him or her before the first child reaches the empty spot in the circle. The tagged child becomes the next IT.

★ Have the children pretend to be monkeys. Choose one child to be the leader who stands in front of the class and performs different motions. The rest of the children mimic the leader. Change leaders often.

Hat Day #3

Feature Focus Read the book *The Hat*.

Learning Labs

★ Have the children make edible "Top Hats." Give each child a piece of lettuce, a pineapple ring, a third of a banana, and some raisins. Show the children how to assemble a hat. Have them place the pineapple ring on top of the lettuce. Then have them stand the banana up inside the pineapple ring. Decorate the hats by sticking raisins into the bananas with toothpicks. Eat as a snack.

★ Leave a supply of precut paper shapes in an art area. Encourage the children to make hat designs out of the shapes. Ask the students to glue the final designs onto pieces of paper.

Think and Talk Time

★ Read the book to the class. Ask the students to describe some of the things they would ask a hat to do if they owned a hat like the one in the book. Brainstorm with the children to create a list of all the different things the hat could do to help people. Ask the children what they think would happen if someone tried to use the hat to do bad things.

Project Pursuits

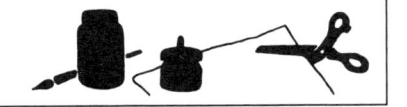

★ Write a class book called "The Further Tales of the Hat." Give each child a hat-shaped piece of paper. Ask them to pretend that they have found the magic hat. Have each child draw a picture of where he or she found the hat on one side of the paper. On the back of the paper, the child should draw a picture that shows how the hat has helped the child. Ask the children to write or dictate narration to accompany their pictures. The narration should be written at the bottom of the pictures. Place the final pictures inside two hat-shaped pieces of construction paper. Write the title on the cover.

★ Have the children make their own paper hats. Show them how to roll a piece of construction paper into a cylinder. Attach each cylinder to a paper plate that has a hole cut out of the center. Decorate with crayons, markers, or scraps of paper.

Movement Models

★ Play "Catch That Hat!" Divide the children into teams. Ask the teams to stand opposite each other on two lines. In the center of the two teams, place a hat. When you call out, "Catch That Hat!" the first child on each team races forward to pick up the hat and take it back to his or her team. The child who does not get the hat may try to tag the other child. If the child is successful, he or she earns a point for that team. If the child with the hat is not caught, he or she earns a point for the team.

★ Play "Where Are the Hats?" Make about twenty hats from colored construction paper. Divide the class into two teams. Have one team leave the room, while the other team hides the hats. Tell the children that a part of each hat must show. Call back the first team and tell them to find the hats. Count to see that all were found. Then reverse the roles of the groups and play again.

Mitten Days

Pattern Page

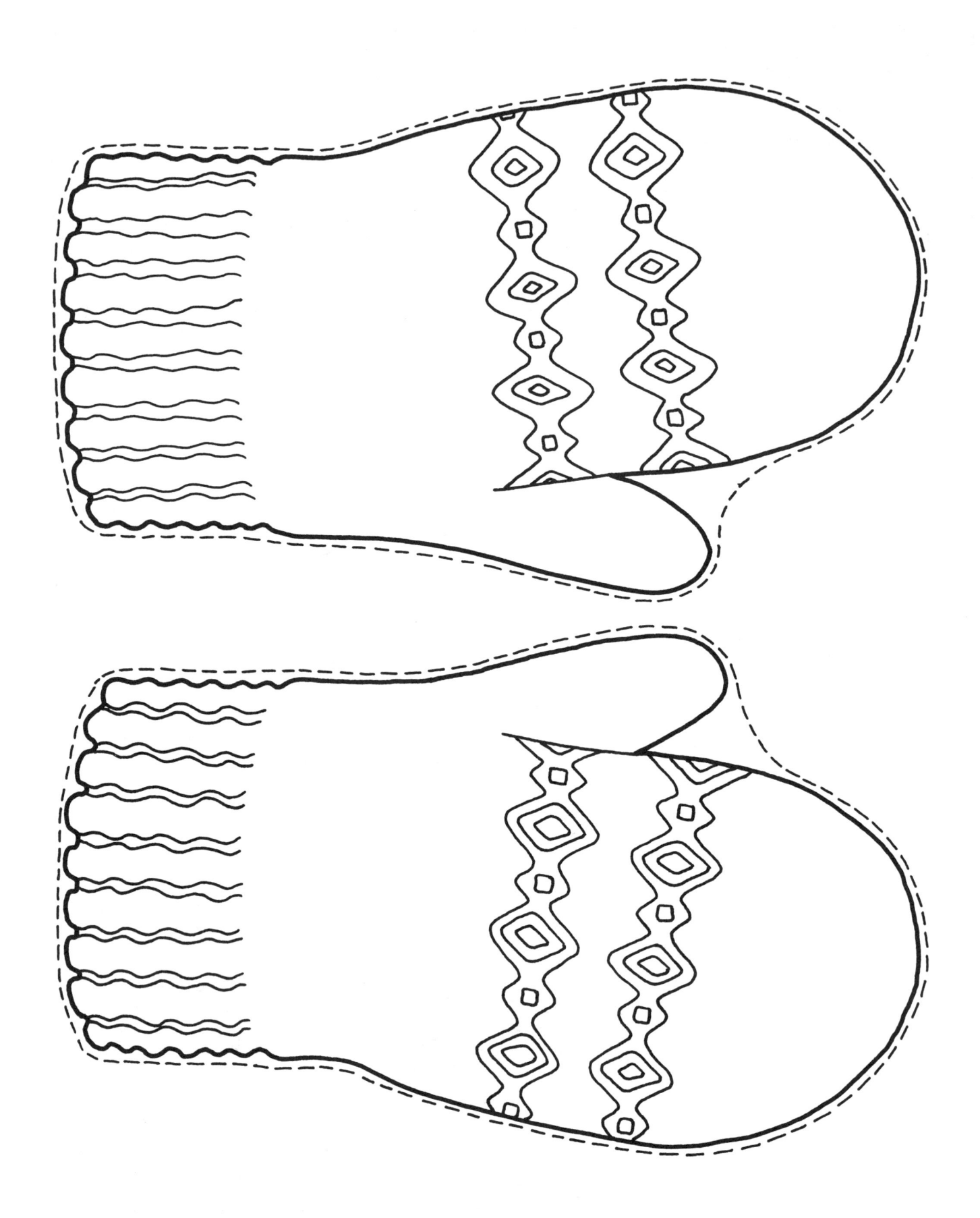

Mitten Days

Timing
   Cold winter day.

What Children Bring
   A pair of mittens or gloves.

Previous Day Reminder
   A small construction-paper mitten pinned to each child's sleeve.

Ready Resources

Books
   Bannon, Laura. *Red Mittens*. Boston: Houghton Mifflin, 1946.
   Galdone, Paul. *Three Little Kittens*. New York: Ticknor & Fields, 1986. (See related activities, page 78.)
   Kellogg, Steven. *The Mystery of the Missing Red Mitten*. New York: Dial Books, 1977.
   Slobodkin, Florence, and Louis Slobodkin. *Too Many Mittens*. New York: Vanguard Press, 1958. (See related activities, page 76.)
   Tresselt, Alvin. *The Mitten*. New York: Lothrop Books, 1964. (See related activities, page 77.)

Poems
   Allen, Marie L. "The Mitten Song." In *A New Treasury of Children's Poetry*. Joanna Cole, ed. New York: Doubleday, 1984.
   Scott, Louise B. "Mittens." In *Rhymes for Learning Times*. Minneapolis, MN: Denison, 1984.

Records and Songs
   Beall, Paula C., and Susan H. Nipp. "Three Little Kittens." In *Wee Sing Nursery Rhymes and Lullabies*. Los Angeles: Price, Stern, Sloan, 1986. (See related activities, page 78.)

Mitten Day #1

Feature Focus Read the book *Too Many Mittens*.

Learning Labs

★ Cut out pairs of red paper mittens. On each pair write a numeral, 1–10. Place in a learning area. Have the children use clothespins to hang matching pairs of mittens on a clothesline.

★ Have students use red crayons to draw around mitten shapes.

Think and Talk Time

★ Have the children classify the mittens they brought from home. You might have them sort the mittens by color, by size, or by design. Discuss the difference between mittens and gloves.

★ Ask the children if they have ever lost mittens. How did they lose the mittens? Did they find them again? Where? Make a list of places where a mitten could be lost. After the discussion, read the story. What happens when one of the children in the books loses a mitten. What happens to all the extra mittens? Brainstorm with the children to create a list of things that could be done with extra mittens.

Project Pursuits

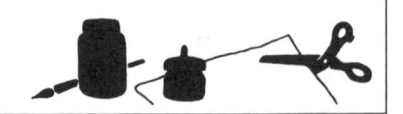

★ Give each child an outline of a pair of mittens. Ask the students to use crayons to make designs on the mittens. Encourage symmetry and image reversal. Have the children add in a background that shows where the mittens might have been found. Hang the final pictures on a clothesline in the classroom.

★ Have the children make "Mitten People." For the body, ask each child to trace around his or her hand on red paper. Remind the children to keep their four fingers together and their thumbs separate as they draw. Have the children cut out the shapes and tape them together, thumbs out. Have the children add a paper-circle head and details. Display on a bulletin board.

Movement Models

★ Play a "Mitten Relay" game with the children. Divide the class into two teams. Have the teams line up facing each other, some distance apart. Give the first child in each team a pair of mittens. When you give a signal, the children must put on the pair of mittens, take them off, and pass them to the next player. When the last player has the mittens on, the team is finished.

★ Play "Drop the Mitten." Ask the children to form a circle. Choose one child to be IT. IT walks around the circle carrying a mitten. At some point, IT drops the mitten behind someone. That person picks up the mitten and chases IT around the circle to the empty spot. If IT is tagged, the person who tagged him or her becomes the new IT. If IT reaches the empty spot without being tagged, he or she remains IT.

Mitten Day #2

Feature Focus Read the book *The Mitten*.

Learning Labs

★ Set up a "What's in the Mitten?" lab. Collect several mittens. In each mitten place a single object. Close the ends of the mittens with rubber bands. Draw a picture of each object you used on a separate index card. Place the mittens and the cards in a learning area. Have each child feel the objects through the mittens and match each mitten with the card that he or she thinks shows the object in the mitten.

★ Draw a picture of each animal in the story. Have the children sequence the animals by size.

Think and Talk Time

★ Discuss different things that could fit in a mitten. Keep a list of the children's suggestions. Then read the story. How did the animals in the story use the mitten? When the boy finds a piece of the mitten, what does he think happened to his mitten? Ask the children if they think all the animals could have really fit into a single mitten. Why or why not?

Project Pursuits

★ Have the children make "Mouse in the Mitten" puppets. Give each child a predrawn mouse (the mouse should fit inside a paper cup), a paper cup, construction paper, and a tongue depressor. Have the children color and cut out the mouse, and glue it to the tongue depressor. Then help the children cover the sides of the paper cups with red construction paper. Add a cutout red paper thumb to turn the cup into a mitten. Cut a small slit in the bottom of each cup so the tongue depressor can fit through the slit. Show the children how to put the mouse in the mitten by putting the puppet into the cup and pushing the depressor through the hole. The children can make the mouse disappear by moving the depressor up and down.

Movement Models

★ Have the children dramatize the story. Use two blankets to represent the mitten. As you read the story, choose different children to act out the parts of animals, and join the other animals in the blankets. When the mitten bursts, have the children jump out of the top blanket and fling it to one side.

★ Play a game called "In-the-Mitten-Tag." Choose one child to be the mouse. Have the rest of the children stand on a goal line. When the mouse calls out "I found a mitten!" the rest of the children try to run to the opposite goal line. When the mouse tags someone, the tagged person becomes another character in the story. He or she must hold hands with the mouse and help the mouse tag other children. Continue playing until nine children have been caught. Then choose a new mouse and start the game again.

Mitten Day #3

Feature Focus Read the book *Three Little Kittens*.
Sing the song "Three Little Kittens."

Learning Labs

★ Draw a picture of a kitten on tagboard. Cut out mitten shapes from different colors of felt. Leave in a learning area. Have the children match pairs of mittens and place one mitten on each hand of the kitten.

★ Let the children cut out and decorate their own mittens of felt or paper.

Think and Talk Time

★ Discuss what it is like to lose mittens with the children. How did their parents react? How did the children feel when they lost a mitten? Read the story to the children. Discuss what the kittens felt like when they lost their mittens. Also discuss what happened when they found their mittens and then soiled the mittens. How did Mother Cat react? Did she react like the children's mothers might?

★ Ask the children to discuss why kittens might need mittens. What type of mittens might they have? What kinds of problems might kittens have with mittens? Tell a story about another animal that decided to buy mittens. Let the children describe the mittens different animals might like.

Project Pursuits

★ Have each child illustrate a scene from the story. Let the children draw their pictures on mitten-shaped pieces of paper. Sequence the pictures and glue them to a long strip of paper. Display in the classroom.

★ Make a class book titled "Where are the Lost Mittens?" Have each child draw or paint a picture that shows where the lost mittens might be. Ask the children to write or dictate a story about the lost mittens and how they got to the location pictured in the illustration. Place the final illustrations inside a piece of folded construction paper and write the title on the cover.

★ Provide the children with yarn, large-eyed blunt needles, and pieces of burlap. Let the children use a running stitch to outline a mitten on the burlap.

Movement Models

★ Play a game called "The Three Little Kittens." Divide the class into groups of three. Have the children who don't make up a full group of three be "lost kittens." (If the class divides evenly, choose three students in one group to be the lost kittens.) Each group of three students should stand single file, each child holding the waist of the child in front of him or her. The lost kittens try to join a group by holding on to the waist of the last child in line. The groups try to maneuver out of the way. If a lost kitten manages to join a group, the first child in line becomes a lost kitten and has to find a new group to join.

★ Have the children dramatize the story in small groups. Supply the children with mittens. Read the story aloud as the children pantomime the action.

Monster Days

Pattern Page

Monster Days

Timing
Halloween
During an alphabet unit

Morning Preview
Play some monster songs to begin the day. (Note: occasionally there may be children who are very afraid of monsters. Be alert to this and do not push these children to participate.)

Ready Resources

Books

Benjamin, Alan. *1000 Monsters*. New York: Scholastic, 1979.
Demarest, Chris L. *Morton and Sidney*. New York: Macmillan, 1987.
Gackenbach, Dick. *Harry and the Terrible Whatzit*. Boston: Houghton Mifflin, 1977.
Haywood, Carolyn. *The King's Monster*. New York: Morrow, 1980.
Kahl, Virginia. *How Do You Hide a Monster?* New York: Scholastic, 1971.
Kent, Jack. *The Scribble Monster*. San Diego, CA: Harcourt Brace Jovanovich, 1981.
Mayer, Mercer. *A Special Trick*. New York: Dial Books, 1976.
_____. *There's a Nightmare in My Closet*. New York: Dial Books, 1976. (See related activities, page 83.)
Parish, Peggy. *Zed and the Monsters*. New York: Doubleday, 1979.
Sendeck, Maurice. *Where the Wild Things Are*. New York: Harper & Row, 1963. (See related activities, page 84.)
Showers, Paul. *A Book of Scary Things*. New York: Doubleday, 1977.
Stone, Jon. *The Monster at the End of This Book*. Racine, WI: Western, 1976.
Willis, Jeanne, and Susan Varlay. *The Monster Bed*. New York: Lothrop Books, 1986.
Willoughby, Elaine M. *Boris and the Monsters*. Boston: Houghton Mifflin, 1986.

Films

Misunderstood Monsters. Los Angeles: Churchill Films, 1981.

Poems

Merriam, Eve. "Five Little Monsters." In *Blackberry Ink*. New York: Morrow, 1983.
Silverstein, Shel. "Monsters I've Met." In *A Light in the Attic*. New York: Harper & Row, 1981. (See related activities, page 82.)

Records and Songs

Sesame Street Monsters. Sesame Street Records. (SSR) 22071.

Monster Day #1

Feature Focus Read the poem "Monsters I have Met."

Learning Labs

★ Make "Monster-Face Toast." Use food coloring to make brightly colored milk. Let each child use a cotton swab and the milk colors to paint a monster face on a slice of white bread. Toast the bread slices. Butter lightly and eat as snacks.

★ Cut out a variety of monster parts from felt. Let students use the parts of make mix-and-match monsters on a flannel board.

Think and Talk Time

★ Discuss monsters with the children. Ask the students questions such as "What is a monster?" "Where might you see one?" "What colors might it be?" Also brainstorm with the children to create a list of places where monsters live and games they might like to play.

★ Read the poem to the children. What types of monsters did the author meet? Have the class tell stories about monsters that they would like to meet. (You may want to point out that monsters are creatures in our imaginations and can be anything that we want them to be.)

Project Pursuits

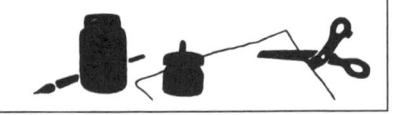

★ Make "Monster Masks" with the children. Give each child a paper bag that will fit over his or her head. Help the children cut out holes for the eyes. Let them use scrap paper, pipe cleaners, fabric, and other materials to make monster faces on their masks. When the masks are finished, divide the class into small groups and have them make up little plays.

★ Let the children make "Monster Mobiles." Give each child a looped strip of cardboard for the base of the mobile. Have them design and cut out four or five monsters. Show them how to use colored yarn to tie the paper monsters to the cardboard strip. Hang the finished mobiles from light fixtures in the classroom.

★ Have the children paint pictures of monsters they would like to meet. Ask each child to dictate or write a few lines about his or her monster. Display under the caption: "Monsters We Would Like to Meet."

Movement Models

★ Play a game called "Monster over the Water." Have the children stand in a circle facing in. Choose one child to be the monster. The monster stands in the center of the circle. Teach the children the chant "Monster over the water, monster over the sea. Monster caught a big fish, but it can't catch *me!*" On the word *me*, the circle of children quickly crouch down. The monster tries to catch someone by tapping him or her on the shoulder before he or she is in a crouch. If a person is tagged, he or she becomes the next monster.

★ Play "Monster Trap." Have the children form a circle. Choose two children to make a bridge or trap by holding their arms together above their heads. Play music as the children form a line and walk under the "monster trap." When the music stops, the children lower their arms and the child under the trap is "caught." Each time two children are caught, they form a new trap next to the starting trap.

Monster Day #2

Feature Focus Read the book *There's a Nightmare in My Closet*.

Learning Labs

★ Have the children make "Monster Salad." Give each child two canned apricot or peach halves. Have them put the fruit on a plate—one piece is the head and the other is the body. Provide raisins, chow mein noodles, or chopped fruit and nuts. Let the children use the materials to make features, arms, and legs on their monsters.

★ Let children paint "Nightmares in Closets." Have the children paint a picture of a "nightmare" with white paint on black paper. Ask each child to tell a few things about his or her drawings.

Think and Talk Time

★ Discuss nightmares with the children. Ask them to tell you different nightmares they have had. Discuss some ways to make nightmares less frightening.

★ Read the book to the class. How did the boy in the story get over being frightened by his nightmare in the closet? Point out that the nightmare might have looked scary, but it turned out to be nice. Have the children discuss scary things that turn out to be nice.

Project Pursuits

★ Make "Nightmare-in-Closet Cards." Help each child cut a "door" in a black piece of construction paper as shown. Then have the children glue the black construction paper onto a piece of white construction paper. Ask them to "open" the door and draw a picture of a nightmare on the white paper. Let the children tell stories about the nightmares in the closets. Then display the pictures on a classroom wall.

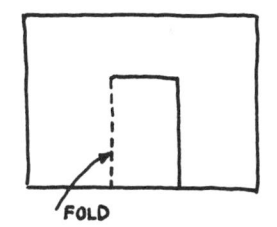

★ Have the class make "Stuffed Monsters." Give each child a large grocery bag. Show them how to stuff the bags with crumpled newspapers. Tie string around the tops of the bags to close. Let the children use paints and fabric to add features to their monsters. Set the finished creatures on a table under the caption: "The Nightmares That Came Out of the Closet."

Movement Models

★ Provide each child with a rope or jump rope. Ask the children to form rectangles with the ropes. Call the rectangles "closets." Give the children directions for movements relative to the "closets." For example, "Jump into the closet," "Jump out of the closet," "Crawl around the closet," "Hop around the closet." Let the children think of other ways of moving relative to the "closet."

★ Play a game called "Nightmare, Nightmare." Ask the children to stand on a goal line in the play area. Choose someone to be the Nightmare, who stands a short distance from the rest of the class. Teach the children to call out, "Nightmare, Nightmare, can we chase you to your lair?" Tell the Nightmare to answer, "Yes, if you are wearing _____ (a color)." All the children wearing that color try to chase the Nightmare. The first child to tag the Nightmare becomes the next Nightmare.

Monster Day #3

Feature Focus   Read the book *Where the Wild Things Are*.

Learning Labs

★ Let children build their own wild things out of pieces of Styrofoam and toothpicks. Spray paint the final creatures after the children are satisfied with their work. Let them glue on pieces of paper for final details.

Think and Talk Time

★ Read the book to the children. Discuss what happens to Max after he is sent to his room. What does his room change into? What types of creatures does he meet? Ask the children to talk about places they would go if they were Max. How would their Wild Things be like Max's? How would theirs be different?

★ Point out that Max became the king of the Wild Things. Discuss the things that Max did as king. Ask the children to describe things that they would like to do if they were kings or queens of the Wild Things. Have the children tell stories about ruling the Wild Things.

Project Pursuits

★ Let the children make "Wild Thing Puppets." Give each child a piece of fake fur, some beads, and other decorative materials. Help the children glue the fur onto a tongue depressor. Add facial features, arms, legs, and tails using the other materials. Let the children put on a puppet show once their puppets are completed.

★ Have the children make a classroom mural showing the places where Wild Things live. Cover a wall with a large piece of butcher paper. Have the children work in pairs along sections of the mural. Ask them to color in a background and glue cutout Wild Things along their stretch of the mural. After the painting is finished, you might have the children take turns telling stories about their trip through the land of the Wild Things.

Movement Models

★ Play a version of "Simon Says" called "Max Says." Tell the children that you will give them a direction. They should only perform the action if you precede your statement by saying "Max Says." If a child performs the action when you have not said "Max Says," that child must say "I'm a Wild Thing," and growl. Play then continues. Make some of your directions silly.

★ Mark two goal lines some distance apart. Ask the children to stand behind one of the lines. Choose someone to be a Wild Thing, who stands facing away from the other children in a "tree" behind the opposite goal line. Tell the children to walk up to the "tree" and call out, "Wild Thing, Wild Thing, come out of the tree. I bet you can't run and catch me!" As the children gather at the "tree," call "Come out!" On this signal, the children race back to the starting line, while the Wild Thing tries to catch them. Those who are caught become the Wild Thing's helpers.

Mud Days

Pattern Page

Mud Days

Timing
　During the rainy season
　During an alphabet unit

What Children Wear
　Old clothes that the children can get dirty.

Previous Day Reminder
　A brown paper shape, with the word *mud* written on it, pinned to each child's shirt.

Ready Resources

Books
Cazet, Denys. *Mud Baths for Everyone.* New York: Bradbury Press, 1981.
Gackenbach, Dick. *Annie and the Mud Monster.* New York: Lothrop Books, 1982.
Grey, Judith. *Mud Pies.* Mahwah, NJ: Troll, 1981.
Nelson, Brenda. *Mud for Sale.* Boston: Houghton Mifflin, 1984.
Pellowski, Michael J. *The Duck Who Loved Mud Puddles.* Mahwah, NJ: Troll, 1986.
Pomerantz, Charlotte. *The Piggy in the Puddle.* New York: Macmillan, 1974. (See related activities, page 89.)
Vigna, Judith. *The Little Boy Who Loved Dirt and Almost Became a Superslob.* Niles, IL: Whitman, 1975.
Wolcott, Patty. *The Marvelous Mud Washing Machine.* Reading, MA: Addison-Wesley, 1974.

Poems
Boyden, Polly C. "Mud." In *A New Treasury of Children's Poetry.* Joanna Cole, ed. New York: Doubleday, 1984.
Lee, Dennis. "The Muddy Puddle." In *The Random House Book of Poetry for Children.* Jack Prelutsky, ed. New York: Random House, 1983. (See related activities, page 89.)
Merriam, Eve. "Dirty Bertie." In *Blackberry Ink.* New York: Morrow, 1985. (See related activities, page 90.)

Records and Songs
Palmer, Hap. "Muddy Water Puddle." On *Sally and the Swinging Snake.* Educational Activities. (AR) 617.
Wayman, Joe, and Don Mitchell. "Mud, Mud, Mud." On *Imagination & Me.* Good Apple. (GA) 48. (See related activities, page 88.)

Short Stories
MacDonald, Betty. "The Radish Cure." In *Mrs. Piggle-Wiggle.* Philadelphia: Lippincott, 1957. (See related activities, page 90.)

Teacher Resources
Wyler, Rose. *Science Fun with Mud and Dirt.* New York: Simon & Schuster, 1986. (See related activities, page 88.)

Mud Day #1

Feature Focus Listen to the song "Mud, Mud, Mud."
Use the resource *Science Fun with Mud and Dirt*.

Learning Labs

★ Take children outside for "Mud Finger Painting." Spread large sheets of heavy butcher paper on a sidewalk or blacktop and tape down. Let the children use gobs of mud to paint designs on the paper.

★ Make "Mud Pudding." Mix 2 tablespoons instant chocolate pudding, 2 tablespoons powdered milk, and 1/3 cup water in 5-ounce paper cups. Chill and eat. (Remind children that they should *not* eat real mud.)

★ Leave brown paint in an art area. Let the children paint "mud" pictures.

Think and Talk Time

★ Listen to the song. Why does the singer like mud? Have children create a list of reasons mentioned in the song. Ask the children if they like mud. Why or why not?

★ Discuss how mud is made. Experiment to see how much water it takes to turn dirt into mud. Have the children measure the numbers of teaspoons of water it takes to turn one cup of dirt into mud. Write a class recipe for mud or mud pies.

Project Pursuits

★ Let the children make "Mud Spatter Paintings." Have each child place a cutout on a piece of white paper. Let them use an old toothbrush and thinned mud or brown paint to spatter paint over the cutout. Help them carefully remove the cutouts and let the picture dry. Display on a classroom wall or bulletin board.

★ Let the children make "Mud Monster Pictures." Have each child tear a shape out of brown construction paper. They should glue the shapes onto drawing paper. Have them add features using markers and scraps of brown paper. Ask each child to write or dictate a few remarks about his or her monster.

★ Use some of the ideas from the resource book to investigate mud and dirt with the children. Help reinforce the idea that mud is dirt mixed with water.

Movement Models

★ Let the children pretend to be playing in the mud. Ask them to pantomime various movements such as walking in deep mud, stepping over or around deep mud puddles, sitting in a mud puddle, making mud pies, and bathing in mud.

★ Play "Mud Ball Toss." Give each child a pair of rolled-up brown socks. Divide the class into teams. Show the children how to throw the socks into empty boxes or wastebaskets. Count the number of times the socks go into the boxes or baskets for each team. Record the numbers for the children to see. Play several rounds of this game.

★ Divide the class into two groups. Play the song again. Have one group march around chanting "mud, mud, mud," while the other group marches around chanting the words of the song.

Mud Day #2

Feature Focus Read the book *Piggy in the Puddle*.
Read the poem "Muddy Puddle."

Learning Labs

★ Cut out puddle shapes from brown construction paper. On each shape write a number. Also cut out pink construction paper pigs. Have the children put the correct number of pigs in each puddle.

★ Let the children mix water and dirt in large flat cake pans to make their own "puddles."

Think and Talk Time

★ Ask the children if they have ever played in mud puddles. Have them describe their experiences. Discuss how their parents reacted to the mud. After the discussion, read the poem. What does the author mean by the "muddiness of mud?"

★ Brainstorm with the children to create a list of animals who like or live in mud. Then read the book. Why did the pig like the mud? How did she convince her parents to join her in the mud? Have the children tell stories about other animals that might like to join the piggy in a puddle.

Project Pursuits

★ Have the children make individual books about playing in the mud. Ask each child to fold a piece of construction paper in half. Have the children draw scenes of different animals doing different things in the mud, such as sitting in a puddle, walking through a puddle, making mud pies, and bathing in mud. Place the completed books inside pieces of folded brown construction paper. Write the title, "Fun in the Mud," on the covers.

★ Have each child draw and cut out a paper pig. Ask the children to use brown crayons to draw a mud puddle and to glue the pig in the puddle. Have the children add details and backgrounds. Display the completed pictures under the caption "Piggies in Puddles."

★ Let the students finger-paint with brown paint that has been mixed with liquid starch. Supply them with slick paper for their paintings.

Movement Models

★ Have a "Puddle Relay Race." Tape irregular brown construction-paper shapes to the floor to make two paths. Divide the class into two teams. One child from each team must run along the path to the end, turn around, run back again, and tag the next child in line without stepping off the path of "puddles."

★ Play "Puddles in the Park." Set out as many carpet squares as there are children. Tell the children that these represent mud puddles in a park. Ask the children to pretend to stroll around the park while they hear music. When the music stops, they must go to a puddle immediately. Only one child may "sit" in a puddle at one time. Each time you begin the music again, remove one puddle. If children do not get to a puddle, they must come and sit by you, pretending they have been sent home to take a bath. Play until there are four or five puddles left.

Mud Day #3

Feature Focus Read the story "The Radish Cure."
Read the poem "Dirty Bertie."

Learning Labs

★ Have students plant red-radish seeds in paper cups. Ask the children to observe the growth.

★ Draw a series of pictures that show a child playing in mud; walking, still muddy, into a bathroom; taking a bath; and being clean. Have students sequence the pictures.

Think and Talk Time

★ Before you begin a discussion, have the children vote on whether or not they enjoy taking baths. Have each child write *yes* or *no* on an index card. Tally the vote by pasting the cards in two columns on a large sheet of paper. After the votes have been counted, ask the children to explain why they feel the way they do.

★ Read the story aloud to the children. Discuss Patty's resistance to taking baths. Ask the students what they think of Mrs. Piggle Wiggle's cure. Do they think their parents would use the Radish Cure if they stopped taking baths? Would it work? Why or why not?

★ Read the poem to the children. Discuss why Bertie would not take a bath. Ask the class to compare Bertie and Patty.

Project Pursuits

★ Point out that the story did not show any pictures of Patty when she was covered with mud and radishes. Ask each child to draw a picture of what he or she thinks Patty looked like just before her bath and just after her bath. Display the final pictures on a bulletin board with the caption "The Radish Cure—Before and After."

★ Have the class make a "Big Book" of the story. Divide the class into groups of two. Each group should decide which events in the story they wish to illustrate. Have the groups of students draw their pictures on 18" × 24" pieces of oak tag. Once the pictures are finished, have each group retell the part of the story they illustrated. Write their narration at the bottom of their picture. Let the whole class decide on the order of the pictures. Punch holes in the side of each picture and insert a binder ring in each hole. Help the class "read" their retold version of the story.

Movement Models

★ Ask the children to pretend to be covered with mud and radishes. Explain that you are going to have them "pull" the radishes out. Call out directions, such as "Pull the radish that is growing on your left knee," or "Pull the radish that is growing on your right ankle." Have the students pantomime the actions.

★ Play a game called "Dirty Bertie and the Mud Monsters." Choose two students to be the Mud Monsters. The rest of the class is Dirty Bertie. Ask the children to stand behind a goal line while the Mud Monsters stand on the other side of the line. When the Mud Monsters call out, "Dirty Bertie, follow me," the children get in line behind either of the Mud Monsters and follows him or her wherever he or she goes. At some point, you call out, "Bath time!" All the children run back toward the goal line. The Mud Monsters try to tag as many children as they can.

Noise Days

Pattern Page

Noise Days

Timing
    Fall
    During a science unit
    During a music unit

What Children Bring
    Any noisy thing.

Previous Day Reminder
    A piece of cardboard with a rubber band around it for each child to take home. (Pluck the band to make a sound.)

Ready Resources

Books

Brown, Margaret W. *The Noisy Book.* New York: Harper & Row, 1939. (See related activities, page 94.)

———. *The Quiet Noisy Boat.* New York: Harper & Row, 1950. (See related activities, page 94.)

Fowler, Richard. *Mr. Little's Noisy Boat.* New York: Putnam, 1986.

Gaeddert, LouAnn. *Noisy Nancy Norris.* New York: Doubleday, 1971.

McCloskey, Robert. *Lentil.* New York: Viking-Penguin, 1978. (see related activities, page 96.)

McGovern, Ann. *Too Much Noise.* Boston: Houghton Mifflin, 1967.

Miles, Miska. *Noisy Gander.* New York: Dutton, 1978.

Moncure, Jane B. *Sounds All Around.* Chicago: Childrens Press, 1982.

Munsch, Robert. *Mortimer.* Toronto, Canada: Annick Press, 1985.

Spier, Peter, *Crash! Bang! Boom!* New York: Doubleday, 1979.

———. *Gobble, Growl, Grunt.* New York: Doubleday, 1979. (See related activities, page 95.)

Thayer, Jane. *Quiet on Account of Dinosaur.* New York: Morrow, 1964.

Wells, Rosemary. *Noisy Nora.* New York: Dial Books, 1980.

Poems

Prelutsky, Jack. "Louder Than a Clap of Thunder." In *New Kid on the Block.* New York: Greenwillow Books, 1984.

Records and Songs

Adventures in Sound. Melody House Recordings. (MH) 55.

Jenkins, Ella. *Play Your Instruments and Make a Pretty Sound.* Folkways/Scholastic. (FLW) 7665. (See related activities, page 96.)

Ustinov, Peter. *Peter and the Wolf.* Angel Records. (ANG) 35638.

Noise Day #1

Feature Focus   Read the books *The Noisy Book* and the *Quiet Noisy Book*.

Learning Labs

★ Make a "Noisy Nook" in a learning area. Display different noisy items for the children to examine. Some objects you might use include glasses filled with different levels of water, different sizes of rubber bands stretched across boxes, bells, whistles, rhythm blocks, and autoharps.

★ Set up a "Noise Match" experiment. Place different objects such as paper clips, dried peas, pennies, and small bells inside opaque cans with lids. For each object, you should have two cans that contain the object. Have the students shake the cans and find the cans with the same objects inside.

★ Make a noisy snack—popcorn. Have children listen to the pops as it cooks and the crunches as they eat.

Think and Talk Time

★ Ask the children to sit quietly with their eyes closed and to listen to the noises around them. What types of noises do they hear? What things could make those noises?

★ Read *The Noisy Book*. Stop before the end of the story. Have the children brainstorm to create a list of possible things the noise could be. Then complete the book and discuss the ending. Repeat using *The Quiet Noisy Book*. What other noises and quiet noises can the children think of? Can some things be both noisy and quiet?

Project Pursuits

★ Make individual or class books titled "Noisy is . . ." or "Quiet is . . ." Have each child draw pictures of things that he or she thinks are noisy or quiet. Ask each child to write or dictate a sentence about the noisy or quiet things he or she has drawn. Place the complete pages inside folded pieces of construction paper and write the title on the cover.

★ Have the children make a "Noisy Bulletin Board." Spread a large piece of butcher paper on the floor. Let the children look through magazines, catalogs, and newspapers for pictures of things that make noise. Have them cut out and glue the pictures onto the butcher paper. Help the children label as many of the pictures as possible. Display on a bulletin board.

Movement Models

★ Ask the children to make all kinds of different noises without using their voices. For example, you might have them clap hands, stomp feet, rub hands, and clap feet. After students have tried the different actions, start a repeating pattern that uses some of the different motions. Have the children follow your lead. Encourage them to create their own rhythm patterns.

★ Have a "Noise Relay." Divide the class into teams. Have the teams stand single file behind a goal line. For each team, on an opposite goal line, place a rattle, a drum with sticks, and two wood blocks. Each child has to run to the objects, shake the rattle, beat the drum once, and hit the two blocks together before running back and tagging the next person in line.

Noise Day #2

Feature Focus Read the book *Gobble, Growl, Grunt.*
Sing the song "Old MacDonald."

Learning Labs

★ Tape different animal sounds on a cassette recorder. Draw or cut out pictures of the different animals that were recorded. Have the students listen to the tape and put the animals in the order that they were recorded.

★ Let the children make different animals out of playdough.

Think and Talk Time

★ Brainstorm with the children to create a list of different animals that make noise. Ask the students to imitate the different noises as you write the animals on the list.

★ Go through the book with the children. Compare the animals in the book to the animals mentioned on the children's list. After sounding out some of the noises in the book, make the sound of three different animals while the children listen to you. Ask the children to identify the animals and then repeat the noises in the same order that you made them. As the children become proficient in this game, increase the number of sounds.

Project Pursuits

★ Have each child draw a picture of an animal that makes a sound. Help the children look in the book and locate the spelling of the sound the animal makes. Have each child copy the sound word onto the bottom of his or her picture. Display on a bulletin board under the heading "Animal Sounds."

★ Let the children make "Animal Paper-Bag Puppets." Provide each child with a small paper lunch bag, construction paper, glue, and scissors. Show the children how to glue paper pieces on the bottom of the bag to create an animal face. The children can manipulate the animals' mouths by opening and closing a hand inside the bags. Have the children use their puppets to put on a play filled with animal sounds, or use the puppets to dramatize the song.

Movement Models

★ Play a game called "Clucks and Peeps." Choose one child to leave the room. This child is the hen. Have the other children sit in a circle. Choose one of these students to be the chick. Ask the hen to return to the circle with closed eyes and say, "Cluck, Cluck." The chick answers by saying, "Peep, Peep." The hen opens his or her eyes and points to whomever he or she thinks made the sound. If the hen is right, the chick becomes the new hen, and the game continues. You can vary this game by using the sounds of other combinations of animals, such as cats and mice, dogs and cows, or sheep and birds.

★ Play the "Animal Noise Game." Ask the children to form a circle holding hands. Choose a leader to stand outside the circle. Using four or five different animal names, assign each child in the circle a particular animal. Choose one of each type of animal to stand in the center of the circle. The leader makes the sound of one of the animals. The children around the circle who have been assigned that animal must change places. The child in the center with that animal name tries to take one of the places.

Noise Day #3

Feature Focus   Read the book *Lentil*.
Listen to the record *Play Your Instruments and Make a Pretty Sound*.

Learning Labs

★ Use thin, strong cord to tie eight to ten nails of different lengths to a rail or table edge. Put the nails in order from shortest to longest. Let the children strike the nails with another nail to create tunes or rhymes.

★ Tape different band instrument sounds for the children to listen to.

★ Show the children how to use a tuning fork. Demonstrate that sound is created by vibrations by striking the fork and placing it in a glass of water. The water will splash as the fork vibrates. Repeat with a tuning fork that has not been struck. Let the children experiment on their own.

Think and Talk Time

★ Read the book to the children. Discuss the different instruments that the band uses. Why did the band members have trouble playing? How did Lentil help? Ask the children if they have ever seen, heard, or played any of the instruments in the band. Have the children tell stories about an instrument that they would like to play.

Project Pursuits

★ Help the children make the following rhythm instruments for a class band:

Kazoo: Let children decorate toilet paper rolls with construction paper and crayons. Help them put waxed paper over one end of each tube and secure with a rubber band. They should hum into the open end.

Tambourine: Let children place several small stones or bottle caps on a heavy-paper plate and tape a second plate over the first. They can decorate the plates and shake them to make noise.

Drum: Have children tape pictures around the outside of a 2-pound coffee can. Place the lid on the can. Children can beat the lid or the sides of the can with a hand or spoon.

Sand Blocks: Help children glue sandpaper onto one side of two wood blocks. They can rub the blocks together to make noise.

Movement Models

★ Have the children listen to some marching music. Then ask the class to clap to the rhythm of the music. After children are comfortable doing this, have them march around the room, walking and clapping in time to the music. Finally, let the children march in time to the music while playing the rhythm instruments they made during *Project Pursuits*. Let the children stand single file and pretend to be a parade marching down the main street of a town.

★ Show the children how to play rhythm instruments softly and loudly. Let them practice for a while, while you direct them. Then show them how to play short sounds and long sounds. Again, let them practice making different sounds. Listen to the instruments on the record, and have the children play in time.

Penguin Days

Pattern Page

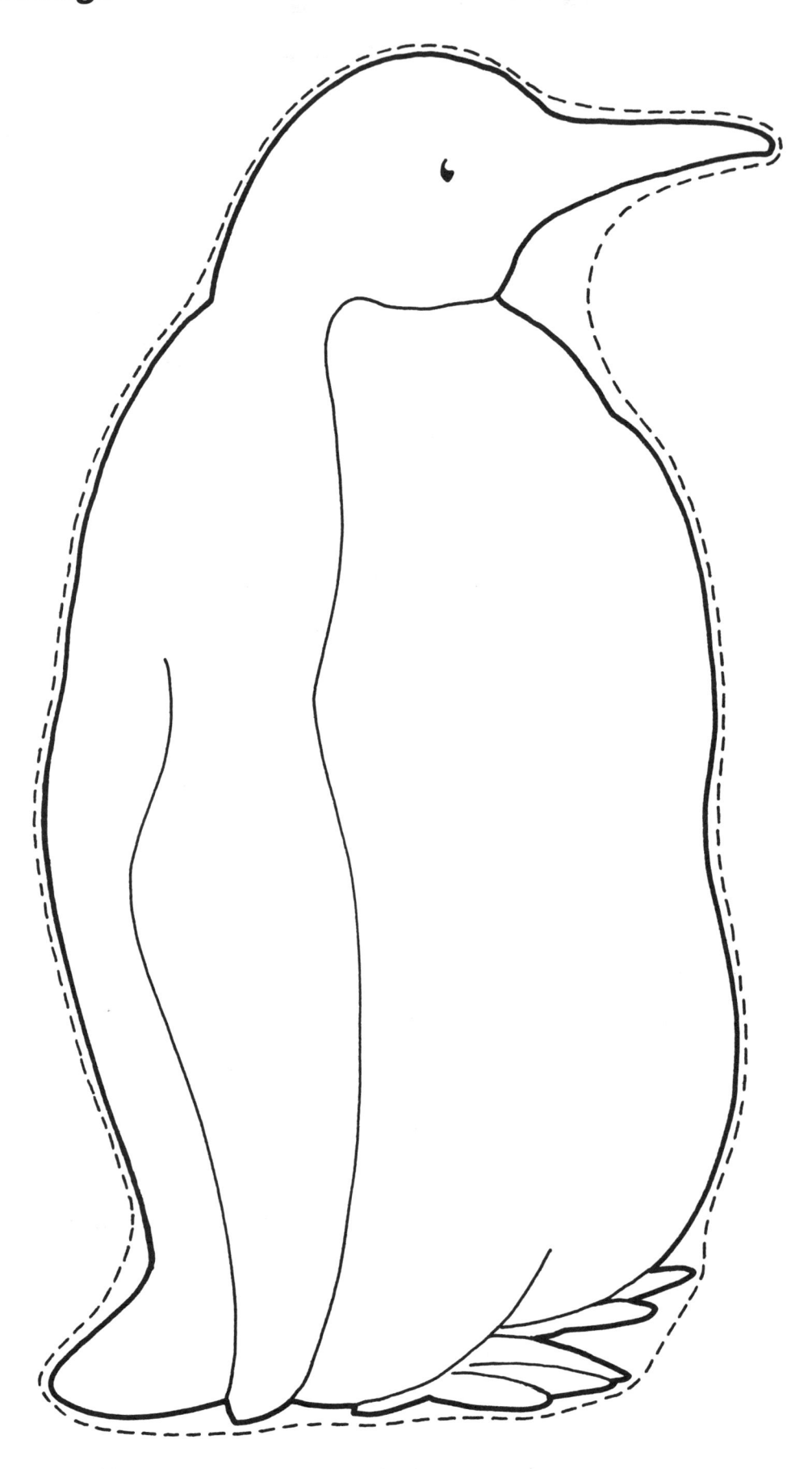

Penguin Days

Timing
   Winter

What Children Wear
   Black and white clothes.

Previous Day Reminder
   Pin a white construction-paper circle with a black dot in the middle onto each child's shirt.

Ready Resources

Books

   Bonners, Susan. *A Penguin Year.* New York: Delacorte, 1981.
   Freeman, Don. *Penguins, Of All People.* New York: Viking-Penguin, 1971. (See related activities, page 101.)
   Hammond, Jane. *Pete the Penguin.* Anderson, IN: Warner Press, 1984.
   Hamsa, Bobbie. *Your Pet Penguin.* Chicago: Childrens Press, 1980. (See related activities, page 102.)
   Hoffman, Mary. *Penguin.* Milwaukee, WI: Raintree, 1985. (See related activities, page 100.)
   Holland, Joyce. *Bessie, The Messy Penguin.* Minneapolis, MN: Denison, 1960.
   Lepthien, Emilie U. *Penguins.* Chicago: Childrens Press, 1983.
   Mizumura, Kazue. *The Emperor Penguin.* New York: Harper & Row, 1969.
   Moskowitz, Stewart. *Fred's Pyramid.* New York: Messner, 1983.
   Penney, Richard L. *The Penguins Are Coming.* New York: Harper & Row, 1969.
   Weiss, Leatie. *Funny Feet.* New York: Avon Books, 1979.
   Whitlock, Ralph. *Penguins.* Milwaukee, WI: Raintree, 1977.
   Winteringham, Victoria. *Penguin Day.* New York: Harper & Row, 1982.

Films

   Perspective Films. *Penguins!* Deerfield, IL: Coronet, 1978. (See related activities, page 100.)

Records and Songs

   Palmer, Hap. "Funky Penguin." On *Movin'.* Educational Activities. (AR) 546.
   ———. "Rag Doll." On *Pretend.* Educational Activities. (AR) 563.

Penguin Day #1

Feature Focus   Watch the film *Penguins!* Read the book *Penguin*.

Learning Labs

★ Let the children measure themselves against a four-foot-high penguin (the actual height of an emperor penguin). Have each child place a black dot next to his or her name on a predrawn graph to show whether he or she is taller, shorter, or the same height as the penguin.

★ Place black and white paint in an art area. Encourage children to paint penguins in snow.

Think and Talk Time

★ Discuss penguins with the class. Try to supplement the discussion with pictures of penguins from magazines and books. Ask the children what they know about penguins. Use the film to show students penguins in action. Point out that penguins are flightless birds, but excellent swimmers. Emphasize the role of penguin parents in daily life. Read the book to give the children more information.

★ Ask the children if they can think of any other flightless birds (ostriches and chickens). Have the children describe things that these birds can do well that flying birds might not be able to do as well.

★ Discuss what it would be like to live at the South Pole. How would the children keep warm? How do penguins keep warm? Point out that the penguins' feathers make their bodies "waterproof" and the layers of fat in their bodies help protect them from the cold.

Project Pursuits

★ Show the class how to draw penguins by making an oval for the body and a circle for the head. Then have the children draw a class mural that shows penguins at the South Pole. Predraw a background on a large sheet of butcher paper. On the left and right sides of the paper, draw "snow" areas. Draw a water area in the middle. Have children add penguins and additional details to the mural. Display on a classroom wall. Let the students tell stories about penguins using the mural for inspiration.

★ Have the children make individual books titled "All About Penguins." Ask each child to fold a piece of construction paper in half and to draw a picture on each page that illustrates a fact about a penguin. Have the children dictate or write sentences about each picture. Place each book inside a piece of folded construction paper.

Movement Models

★ Let the children pretend to be penguins walking on ice. Show them how to do the penguin walk—arms straight down at sides, knees straight, head forward, and body moving side to side. You might also let them pretend to be emperor penguins carrying their babies on their feet. Give each child a soft beanbag to place on his or her feet. Ask the children to try to walk short distances without losing the beanbag.

★ Play "Penguins in the Sea." Mark off two boundaries in the play area. Explain that the children are penguins swimming in the ocean and that they have to swim from one boundary to the other by running. Choose one child to be a leopard seal. The leopard seal stands between the two boundaries and tries to tag the penguins as they run from one side to the other. Any penguin that is tagged is frozen in place. Penguins outside the lines also become frozen. Play until half the penguins are frozen.

Penguin Day #2

Feature Focus Read the book *Penguins, Of All People.*

Learning Labs

★ Create a "South Pole" role-playing area in a drama area. Drape white sheets over the area and let the children pretend to be penguins in the snow.

★ Cut out and color 5–10 penguins of different sizes and leave in a learning area for the children to sequence.

Think and Talk Time

★ Discuss peace with the children. Ask questions such as, "What is peace?" "Can we do anything to help keep peace?" "Why is peace important?" After the discussion read the book. How does Peary P. Penguin promote peace? Was his advice to the U.N.—have fun, work together, play together, and be a family—good advice? Why or why not? Discuss ways to use this advice at home, in school, and in the world.

★ Have the children pretend that Peary and Polly Penguin have twins—a boy and a girl. They want to name their children names that start with the letter "P." Have the children brainstorm to create a list of names that start with "P." Vote to decide on the best names for the twins.

★ Discuss personification with the class. What human traits do the penguins in the book have? Ask the children to compare real penguins to those in the book.

Project Pursuits

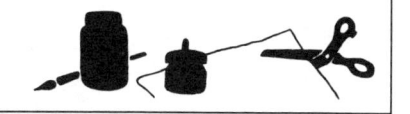

★ Have the children make "Peary's Peace Posters." Ask them to illustrate ways in which they could use Peary's advice at school. Display the posters on a wall along with another poster that lists Peary's advice.

★ Let the children make "Peary or Polly Penguin Puppets." Supply each child with a paper lunch bag, black and white construction paper, and glue. Show children how to cut out penguin body parts from black and white paper. Ask each child to glue a paper beak and eyes on the bottom of the bag to create a penguin face. Yellow feet made from scrap paper could be glued to the edge of the bag.

Movement Models

★ Play a game called "Pin the Medal on Peary." Cut out a penguin from black paper. Add a white front. Also make a medal by gluing a yellow construction paper circle to a piece of ribbon. Tape the penguin to a wall where children can reach it. Blindfold a child and ask him or her to pin the medal to Peary's chest. Let all the children have a chance.

★ Play a version of "Duck, Duck, Goose," called "Duck, Duck, Penguin." Ask the children to sit in a circle. Choose one child to go around the circle tapping each child, saying "Duck." At some point, the child should tap someone and say, "Penguin." Both the tapper and the tapped child do a penguin walk around the circle, the tapped child trying to tag the tapper before the tapper reaches the empty spot in the circle. If the child is tagged, he or she remains the tapper.

Penguin Day #3

Feature Focus Read the book *Your Pet Penguin*.

Learning Labs

★ Write simple math problems on penguin cutouts. Also cut out brown paper fish. Leave the penguins and the fish in a learning center. Have children count out the correct number of fish for each penguin.

★ Provide the children with black and white playdough in an art area. Encourage the children to make different sizes of penguins.

Think and Talk Time

★ Show the children pictures of penguins in books or magazines. Ask the children to pretend that they have the opportunity to get a baby penguin as a pet. How would they convince their parents that a penguin would make a good pet? What are some of the reasons that their parents might give for not wanting a penguin around the house? Keep a list of the children's suggestions.

★ Read the book to the class. Why does the author think a penguin would make a good pet? Why does the author think a penguin would make a bad pet? Compare the reasons in the book with the children's list of reasons.

★ Have the children make up stories about receiving a penguin as a birthday present. What would they feed it? Where would it live? What kinds of games could they play with a penguin?

Project Pursuits

★ Give each child a precut penguin shape to incorporate into a picture. Ask the children to illustrate a scene that shows what it would be like to have a pet penguin. Have them add in features and backgrounds with markers or crayons. After the pictures are finished, have each child write or dictate a few sentences about the picture. Display on a classroom wall or bulletin board.

★ Use fish-shaped crackers to create math problems for the class. Pass out crackers to each child. Then tell the class a story. For example, you might say, "Your pet penguin had four fish." (Have the children count out four crackers.) "Then the penguin ate two fish." (Have the children eat two crackers.) "How many fish does your penguin have left?" Continue using the crackers to create more addition and subtraction problems.

Movement Models

★ Play a game called "My Pet Penguin Says." Tell the children to stand like penguins—arms held straight down, knees straight, head facing forward. Explain that you will give them a direction. They should only perform the action if you precede your directions by saying, "My pet penguin says." Ask the children to make motions such as walking backward, waddling in circles, flapping wings, and bobbing heads.

★ Play "Feed the Penguin." Tape a large piece of paper to the floor. Draw three or four large penguins on it. On each penguin's chest, write a numeral. Let the children take turns "feeding the penguins" by tossing "fish" (tan beanbags) onto the penguins. Tell the children to keep track of the points they get by counting out paper clips. At the end of the game, ask the children to count their paper clips.

Pocket Days

Pattern Page

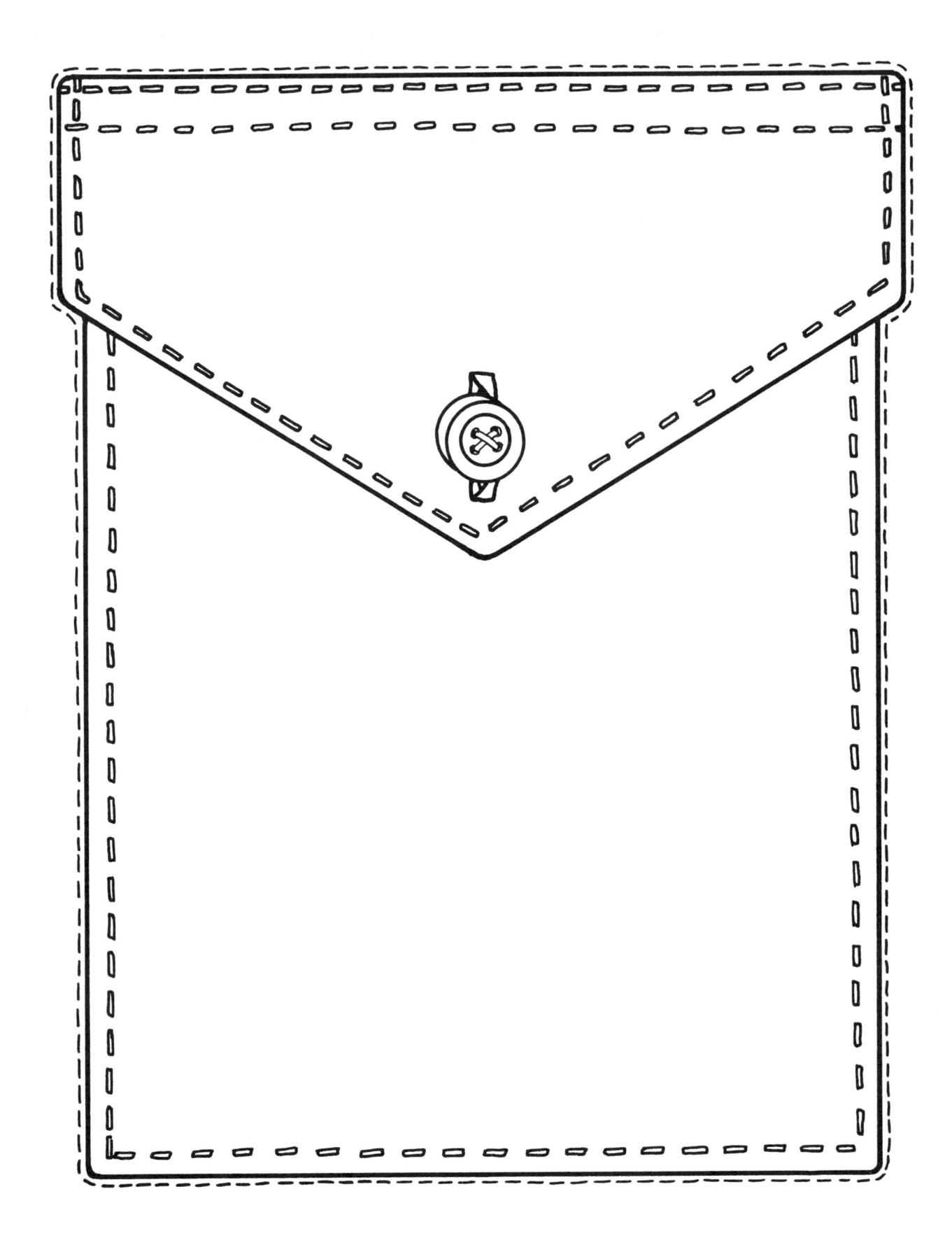

Pocket Days

Timing
   Spring
   Anytime

What Children Bring
   Something in a pocket.

Previous Day Reminder
   A pocket shape cut from construction paper pinned to each child's shirt.

Ready Resources

Books
   Barrett, Judith. *Peter's Pocket.* New York: Atheneum, 1974. (See related activities, page 107.)
   Caudill, Rebecca. *A Pocketful of Cricket.* New York: Holt, Rhinehart & Winston, 1964. (See related activities, page 106.)
   Foster, Doris V. *A Pocketful of Seasons.* New York: Lothrop Books, 1960. (See related activities, page 106.)
   Freeman, Don. *A Pocket for Corduroy.* New York: Viking-Penguin, 1978.
   Merriam, Eve. *What Can You Do With a Pocket?* New York: Knopf, 1964. (See related activities, page 108.)
   Miles, Miska. *Gertrude's Pocket.* Magnolia, MA: Peter Smith, 1984.
   Payne, Emmy. *Katy No-Pocket.* Boston: Houghton Mifflin, 1973. (See related activities, page 107.)

Poems
   De Regniers, Beatrice S. "Keep a Poem in Your Pocket." In *Random House Book of Poetry for Children.* Jack Prelutsky, ed. New York: Random House, 1983.
   Merriam, Eve. "Something in My Pocket." In *Blackberry Ink.* New York: Morrow, 1984.

Records and Songs
   Wayman, Joe. "Robert's Pocket." On *If You Promise Not to Tell.* Good Apple. (GA) 625.

Pocket Day #1

Feature Focus Read the book *A Pocket Full of Cricket* or *A Pocketful of Seasons*.

Learning Labs

★ Make "Pocket Sandwiches" with the class. Cut pita bread into halves or quarters. Let the children stuff the "pockets" with tuna salad, cheese, or peanut butter. Eat for snacks.

★ Glue library card pockets inside a file folder. On the outside of each pocket, write a letter. On index cards, glue cutout pictures that start with the same letters as you wrote on the pockets. Make several picture cards for each letter. Have the children place each card in the appropriate pocket.

★ Mount four old jean pockets on oak tag. Above each pocket, draw or glue a picture of a seasonal scene. Place the board and a variety of seasonal objects in a learning area. Have the children put each object into the correct pocket.

Think and Talk Time

★ Have the children count the number of pockets they have on their clothing. Record the data on a bar graph for the class. Ask the children if any of the pockets are in unusual places. Point out that some pockets have flaps or buttons, while other pockets are plain.

★ Let the children share the objects in their pockets. Then brainstrom with the class to create a list of objects that could be kept in a pocket. Read one of the books to the class.

Project Pursuits

★ Make a classroom bulletin board with the children. Cut out a large shirt, a skirt, and a pair of pants from construction paper. Pin to a bulletin board. Have each child make a pocket to fit on the clothing. Ask each child to draw and cut out an object to put in his or her pocket. Let the children pin their pockets to the boards and put the objects inside. Add a caption which reads, "Full Pockets."

★ Have the children make individual books. Ask each child to fold a piece of construction paper in half. For each page of the book, the child should draw and cut out a pocket and something that he or she would like in the pocket. Have the children glue the pockets to the pages and place the objects in the pockets. Ask the children to write or dictate a few remarks about the objects on each page. Place each book inside a piece of folded construction paper. Write a title on the cover.

Movement Models

★ Have the children pretend to be different objects that are found in pockets, such as a cricket, a bouncing Super Ball, a curled-up snail shell, or a hopping frog.

★ Provide each child with a jump rope or string. Show the children how to form "pocket" shapes with the ropes. Give directions for movements relative to the pockets, such as "Crawl into the pocket," "Hop out of the pocket," "Walk around the pocket," "Jump in and out of the pocket three times."

★ Play a game called "Ball in the Pocket." Ask the children to form a circle. Give the children three or four balls. Explain that the children represent a pocket. Let the children roll the balls inside the pocket. The students may use their hands or feet to keep the balls from rolling outside the pocket, but the children must remain in place. If a ball rolls outside the circle, the children must leave it. Play until all the balls are lost.

Pocket Day #2

Feature Focus   Read the book *Katy No-Pocket* or *Peter's Pocket*.

Learning Labs

★ Cut out shirt shapes from different colors or patterns of fabric or wallpaper. Glue each shirt to a piece of tagboard. Also cut out pocket shapes from the same pieces of fabric or wallpaper. Leave the shirts and the pockets in a learning area. Have the children place each pocket on the corresponding shirt.

Think and Talk Time

★ Have the children share the objects they brought from home. Ask the children to consider what it would be like if there were no pockets. Discuss how this would affect the children. How would it affect clowns? Farmers? Carpenters?

★ Read one of the books. Why did the main character need a pocket? What did each do to get a pocket? Ask the children to think of other ways that Katy or Peter could have gotten pockets.

★ Brainstorm with the children to create a list of objects that Katy or Peter could put in their pockets. If the children could wish for one special thing to appear in their pockets, what things would they wish for?

Project Pursuits

★ Let the children draw a picture of someone that they think needs a pocket. Give each student a precut pocket to add to the drawing. Ask the students to write or dictate a story about how the person got a pocket. Display on a classroom wall or bulletin board.

★ Let the students make "Lace-Up Pockets" for their parents. Provide the students with precut pocket shapes made from tagboard. Help the children punch holes in the pockets. Let them use a large-eyed blunt needle to lace two pocket pieces together as shown.

After the pockets are finished, have the class make "job" coupons for jobs that the children will do for their parents. Put the coupons in the pockets.

Movement Models

★ Play "Pick a Pocket." Wear a carpenter's apron or some other piece of clothing that contains many pockets. Place task cards in the pockets that direct students to do different movements, such as hopping, skipping, jumping, and stretching. Each student picks a card out of a pocket. Read each card aloud to the students and have them perform the action.

★ Play a game called "Pass the Pocket." Divide the class into three or four equal teams. Have each team sit in a circle. Give a paper pocket to one child on each team. At a starting signal, the children start to pass the pocket around the circle—receiving the pocket with one hand and passing it with the other. When the pocket reaches the starting child, that child walks to a chalkboard and makes a tally mark for his or her team. Then he or she returns to the circle and starts passing the pocket again. The game continues until one team has five tally marks.

Pocket Day #3

Feature Focus Read the book *What Can You Do With a Pocket?*

Learning Labs

★ Cut five pocket shapes out of construction paper. Cut a window in the center of each pocket. Tape a piece of clear plastic behind each window. Tape or glue the sides and bottom of each pocket onto a piece of tagboard. Draw or glue a picture of a community helper—such as a carpenter, a nurse, a baker, a teacher, and a repairman—above each pocket. Draw pictures of tools that each helper uses on separate cards. Place in a learning area. Have the children put the correct tools in each pocket.

★ Leave clothes with lots of pockets in the creative play area for the children to use.

Think and Talk Time

★ Wear an apron that has several pockets. Place some of the items mentioned in the book in the pockets. Remove the items one-by-one and ask the children to tell you who might use the item and how the person would use it. Read the book.

★ Have the children share the items in their pockets. When appropriate, encourage the class to think of different ways that the items could be used.

Project Pursuits

★ Have the students make "Pocket Puppets." Give each child a library card pocket that has a small slit in the bottom. Ask each student to draw and cut out a person or animal to fit in the pocket. Have the children glue a Popsicle stick to the backs of their figures. Let the children decorate the pockets, then show them how to place the figure inside the pocket by pushing the stick through the slit. The children can manipulate the figures by moving the sticks up and down.

★ Let the children make "Pocket Ponchos" for their favorite stuffed toys. Give each child a 12"-square piece of fabric that has a 3" slit in the middle, and a 2½" white fabric pocket. Let the students decorate the pockets with fabric markers. Then help them glue the pockets onto the ponchos. Slip the head of the toy through the slit.

Movement Models

★ Have the students run "Pocket Relays." Divide the class into teams. Give each team an old pillowcase (a pocket). Show the children how to get in the pillowcase and hop. Have each child hop to a goal line, step out of the "pocket," run back to his or her team, and hand the "pocket" to the next child in line.

★ Play "Fill the Pocket." Divide the class into teams. Have each team stand in a row. Give the first child in each team a lunch bag (the pocket) containing a variety of items such as a tennis ball, a toothpick, and a pencil. Give the last child in each row an empty lunch bag. At a signal, the first child in each row pulls the objects, one at a time, from the bag and passes them to the next child. The objects get passed down the row to the last child, who places them into the empty "pocket." When all of the objects have been passed down the line, the last child sends them back, one at a time, to the first child.

Scarecrow Days

Pattern Page

Scarecrow Days

Timing
    Fall
    Halloween

What Children Wear
    Scarecrow costumes.

Previous Day Reminder
    A piece of straw in a sandwich bag.

Ready Resources

Books

Baum, Frank L. *The Wizard of Oz*. New York: Random House, 1984.
Farber, Norman. *There Goes Feathertop!* New York: Dutton, 1979.
Gordon, Sharon. *Sam the Scarecrow*. Mahwah, NJ: Troll, 1980.
Miller, Edna. *Pebbles: A Pack Rat*. Englewood Cliffs, NJ: Prentice-Hall, 1976. (See related activities, page 114.)
Oana, Katy. *Robbie and the Raggedy Scarecrow*. Moore Haven, FL: Rainbow Books, 1978.
Potter, Beatrix. *The Tale of Benjamin Bunny*. Mineola, NY: Dover, 1974.
The Unscary Scarecrow. New York: Outlet Book Company, 1985. (See related activities, page 113.)

Films

Scarecrow Man. Peru, IL: Educational Media Associates, 1973.

Poems

Scott, Louise B. "Scarecrow." In *Rhymes for Learning Times*. Minneapolis, MN: Denison, 1983.

Records and Songs

Bolger, Ray. "If I Only Had a Brain." On *The Wizard of Oz*. Caedmon Records. (CAE) TC–1512.

Short Stories

Anderson, Paul S. "The Scarecrow." In *Story Telling with the Flannel Board*, Book 2. Minneapolis, MN: Denison, 1970. (See related activities, page 112.)

Scarecrow Day #1

Feature Focus   Read the story "The Scarecrow."

Learning Labs

★ Cut out scarecrow shirts from different colors of construction paper. Also cut out an equal number of blackbird shapes from white paper. Write the names of the colors you used for the shirts on the blackbirds. Place in a learning center. Have children match each shirt with the corresponding blackbird.

Think and Talk Time

★ Discuss scarecrows with the children. Why are there scarecrows? Where might you find a scarecrow? How do they help farmers? Brainstorm with the children to create a list of unusual places where they might find a scarecrow. Read the story.

★ Let the children share their scarecrow costumes. Have each child stand in front of the class and pretend to be a scarecrow in a field. The rest of the class asks the child questions such as, "Where do you work?" and "What types of things do you see where you work?" Have each child tell you about something that he or she scared away. Keep a list of the children's answers. Encourage them to think of unique things to "scare."

Project Pursuits

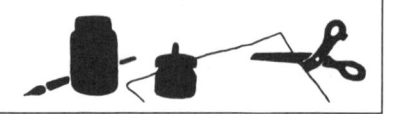

★ Help the children make a real scarecrow for the classroom. Use an old mop, and nail a board across the center for arms. Place clothes over the mop and board. Let the children help you stuff the clothes with crumpled newspapers. Attach a cardboard face under the mop "hair" and place a hat over the top. If you wish, tie straw to the wrists and ankles of the scarecrow to give the look of straw stuffing. Have the class vote on the best name for their scarecrow.

★ Have the children draw pictures that show scarecrows in unusual places. Encourage the children to include themselves in the pictures. Ask each child to write or dictate a story about the scarecrow. The stories should be written below the pictures. Display on a classroom wall or bulletin board.

Movement Models

★ Play "Scarecrow Tag." Teach the children the following song (to the tune of "Down by the Station"):

> Out in the cornfield, early in the morning, stands a lonely scarecrow, chasing crows away. See the blackbirds scurry, they are in a hurry, flap, flap, caw, caw, off they go!

Choose one child to be the scarecrow. The rest of the children are crows. The scarecrow stands in the middle of a circle drawn on the floor. This circle is the field. All the children sing the song, and as they sing, the crows move into the field. On the word "go," the scarecrow starts to chase the crows, trying to tag them before they reach a designated safe area. As the crows are tagged, they sit in a row out of the action. After eight crows have been caught, a new scarecrow is chosen and the game begins again.

Scarecrow Day #2

Feature Focus   Read the book *The Unscary Scarecrow*.

Learning Labs

★ Place uncooked popcorn pieces or paper ears of corn in a math center. Let the children use the pieces for counting, forming sets, and matching objects to numbers.

★ Cut scarecrow figures and hats out of construction paper. On each scarecrow write a numeral, 1–10. On each hat, draw a corresponding number of dots or shapes. Leave in a learning center. Have the children place the corresponding hat on each scarecrow. Colored stick-on dots on the the back of each piece makes this game self-correcting.

★ Place straw hats, plaid shirts, and overalls in the creative play area. Let the children pretend to be scarecrows in a field.

Think and Talk Time

★ Discuss a scarecrow's job. What is a scarecrow supposed to do? What would be best about the job? What would be worst?

★ Read the book to the children. Why wasn't the scarecrow scary? Why was this a problem? Have the children tell stories about what it would be like to be a scarecrow who couldn't scare the crows. What other pests should a scarecrow be able to scare?

Project Pursuits

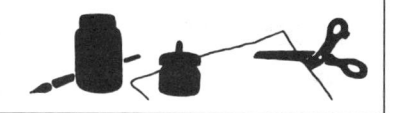

★ Have the children paint "Scarecrows in Gardens." Provide the children with paint and sponges. Show them how to use the sponges and paint to paint pictures of gardens. Once the paintings have dried, give each child a precut shirt, pants, and hat to add to the painting. Have them add features and details with crayons or markers. Encourage children to tell something about their paintings. Display in the classroom.

★ Make a classroom bulletin board. Have each child draw and cut out a picture of a scarecrow. Pin to a bulletin board. Add construction-paper corn stalks. Place the caption, "The Unscary Scarecrows" on the board above the display.

★ Have the children draw pictures of things they might see if they were a scarecrow in a garden. Have each child write or dictate a few sentences about his or her picture. The comments should be written at the bottom of the pictures.

Movement Models

★ Dramatize one scene from the story. Read the story aloud and pick children to act out the different parts in the scene. Change players until everyone has had a chance to participate.

★ Play a game called "The Scarecrow and the Crows." Ask the children to form a circle. Choose four children to be "crows." These children stand in the center of the circle. Choose another child to be the scarecrow. This child stands outside the circle. When you call out, "Scare the Crows!" the scarecrow enters the circle and tries to tag all the crows. The crows cannot run outside the circle. As the crows are tagged, they join the other children in the circle. The last child to be caught becomes the next scarecrow, and the play continues.

Scarecrow Day #3

Feature Focus Read the book *Pebbles: A Pack Rat*.

Learning Labs

★ Draw and cut out a large cardboard scarecrow. Glue several library card pockets on the front of the figure. Cut out the same number of rat shapes from construction paper. Write a capital letter on the front of each pocket. On each pack rat, write a corresponding lower-case letter. Leave in a learning center. Have the children put each pack rat in the appropriate pocket.

★ Leave paints and brushes in a creative art area. Have the children paint pictures of scarecrows. If possible, pin up pictures of real scarecrows in the area for inspiration.

Think and Talk Time

★ Ask the children if they know what a pack rat is. Explain the term, then read the story. Discuss the scarecrow in the book. How did the scarecrow feel about Pebbles living in his clothing? How did the scarecrow feel at the end of the story? Encourage the children to tell stories about what might happen the day after the story ends.

Project Pursuits

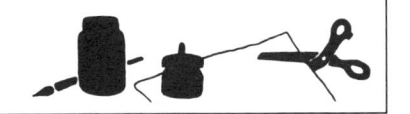

★ Play "Build a Scarecrow." Draw several scarecrows, each on a separate piece of oak tag. Cut each figure into six pieces—a head, a body, two arms, and two legs. Then write the following numbers on each body part, using a different color for each scarecrow: 1—head, 2—body, 3—right arm, 4—left arm, 5—right leg, 6—left leg. Divide the class into groups. Give each group a set of scarecrow pieces and a number cube. Students "build" their scarecrows by rolling the number cube and taking the scarecrow piece that matches the number on the cube. Scarecrows must be built in numerical order. If the students don't get the number they need, they must keep rolling until it appears. Play continues until one group has completed their scarecrow.

★ Let the children glue precut geometric shapes on pieces of paper to make scarecrows. Ask the children to use markers or crayons to add in details and background.

Movement Models

★ Play a game called "Stuff the Scarecrow." Draw scarecrow faces on paper grocery bags. Provide the children with rolled-up pairs of socks or crumpled newspaper balls. Place the opened bags some distance from the children. Have them "stuff" a scarecrow by throwing the balls into the bag. Ask the children to keep track of how many balls they get into the bags by making tally marks on the chalkboard.

★ Play "Pebbles in the Scarecrow." Choose someone to be Pebbles. Ask the rest of the children to form a circle and hold hands. They represent the scarecrow. Pebbles stands in the center of the circle. The rest of the children chant, "Pebbles, Pebbles, we won't let you out, until the farmer comes and gives a shout!" On the word "farmer," the children in the circle hold their hands up in arches. Pebbles tries to escape before the children put their arms down again on the words, "a shout!"

Squirrel Days

Pattern Page

Squirrel Days

Timing
  Fall

Morning Preview
  Before class, hide nuts around the room. When children come in, tell them to pretend to be squirrels on a nut hunt. Ask them to find as many nuts as they can in five minutes. If you wish, you can also have the students tell you where they found the nuts.

Ready Resources

Books
  DeLage, Ida. *The Squirrel's Tree Party.* Easton, MD: Garrard, 1978.
  Fremlin, Robert. *Three Friends.* New York: Dell, 1976.
  Lane, Margaret. *The Squirrel.* New York: Dial Books, 1982. (See related activities, page 118.)
  Peet, Bill. *Merle, The High Flying Squirrel.* Boston: Houghton Mifflin, 1974.
  Potter, Beatrix. *The Tale of Squirrel Nutkin.* New York: Bantam, 1984.
  Schumaker, Claire. *Nutty's Birthday.* New York: Morrow, 1986.
  _____. *Nutty's Picnic.* New York: Morrow, 1986.
  Sharmat, Majorie. *Sophie and Gussie.* New York: Macmillan, 1976.
  Wolkstein, Diane. *Squirrel's Song.* New York: Knopf, 1976. (See related activities, page 120.)
  Wormer, Joe V. *Squirrels.* New York: Dutton, 1978.
  Zion, Gene. *The Meanest Squirrel I Ever Met.* New York: Atheneum, 1982. (See related activities, page 119.)

Films
  Gray Squirrel. Chicago: Encyclopedia Britannica Educational Corporation, 1961. (See related activities, page 118.)
  Squirrel on My Shoulder. Chicago: Films, Inc., 1981.
  Where Should a Squirrel Live? Pasadena, CA: Barr Films, 1971.

Poems
  Scott, Louise B. "Andilla." In *Rhymes for Learning Times.* Minneapolis, MN: Denison, 1983.
  "The Squirrel." In *Piping Down the Valleys Wild.* Nancy Larrick, ed. New York: Delacorte Press, 1985.
  Yeats, William Butler. "To a Squirrel at Kyle-Na-No." In *Piping Down the Valleys Wild.* Nancy Larrick, ed. New York: Delacorte Press, 1985.

Records and Songs
  "Squirrel Nutkin." In *Sing Through the Days.* Society of Brothers. Rifton, NY: Plough, 1969.

Squirrel Day #1

Feature Focus Read the book *The Squirrel* or watch the film *Gray Squirrel*.

Learning Labs

★ Cut out squirrels from construction paper. Make pairs of tails out of different textures of fabric. Glue one tail on each squirrel. Place the squirrels in a learning center. Have children feel the tails and match the squirrels that have the same textured tails.

★ Collect acorns with the children. Use them in a math center for counting or forming sets.

Think and Talk Time

★ Start a discussion about squirrels by reading the book or watching the film. Ask children to describe what squirrels are like: Where do they live? What do they eat? What are their daily lives like?

★ Take the children on a field trip to observe squirrels. Ask the children to observe how the squirrels interact with each other. Discuss how a squirrel's life changes during the different seasons.

★ Once you are back in the classroom, ask the children to tell stories about games that the squirrels might play or things that they might say to each other. If you wish, record the stories to make a class book.

Project Pursuits

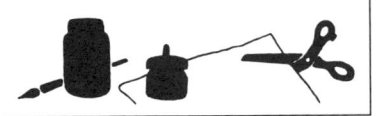

★ Give each student a squirrel sticker to incorporate into an illustration. Ask the students to draw a picture that shows something the squirrel might do as part of his or her daily routine. Have the children write or dictate narrative to accompany the picture. Display the pictures and narration on a bulletin board.

★ Play a game called "The Squirrel's Nuts." Make a 9" × 12" card for each child. On each card, draw a squirrel and a set of six acorns. Print a color word on each acorn. Use a variety of words so each card has a different set of words. Cut out colored paper acorns to match all the color words. Place these within reach of the children. Prepare a spinner with the color words in sections around it. Have the children take turns spinning the spinner, reading the word it lands on, and looking at their set of acorns for the word. If they find it, they cover it with the appropriately colored paper acorn.

Movement Models

★ Play a game called "The Squirrel and the Nut." Have the children stand in a circle, cupping their hands behind them. Choose one child to be the squirrel. Give this child a nut or a cork representing a nut. The squirrel walks around the circle and puts the nut into another child's hands. This child chases the squirrel and tries to tag him or her before he or she reaches the empty spot in the circle. The child who receives the nut is the next squirrel.

★ Play "Squirrels and Trees." Divide the children into groups of three. In each group, two children join hands to form a "tree." The third child, the squirrel, stands between them. Choose a child to be IT. IT calls out, "Squirrels, hunt for nuts!" All the squirrels leave their trees and walk around the play area. At some point, you should call out, "Squirrels, go home!" Then all the squirrels run to an empty tree. IT also tries to find a tree. Whoever is caught without a tree becomes the next IT.

Squirrel Day #2

Feature Focus   Read the book *The Meanest Squirrel I Ever Met*.

Learning Labs

★ Make "Peanut Butter Nuts" with the class. Let the children mix 1 cup peanut butter, ½ cup powdered sugar, and ½ cup condensed milk in a bowl. Show the children how to roll the mixture into small balls. Let the children pretend to be squirrels as they nibble on their "nuts."

★ Draw a picture of a squirrel on a piece of tagboard. On index cards, write a numeral 1–10. Place the board and the cards in a math area, along with peanuts in the shell or acorns. Have the child draw a card, read the number, and place the correct number of peanuts or acorns on the squirrel.

★ Create a "Nut Tree Restaurant" role-playing area. Provide the children with a menu, some nuts in the shell, some small baskets, and a table.

Think and Talk Time

★ Brainstorm with the children to create a list of ways in which a squirrel might be "mean." Read the book. Compare the students' responses with M.O. Squirrel's actions. What made M.O. Squirrel change his ways?

★ Point out the restaurant menu in the book. Ask the children to think of some other foods that contain nuts. Create a menu for a squirrel cafe with the class. Ask them to name the cafe. Discuss what it would be like to eat only nuts.

Project Pursuits

★ Make acorn-shaped books for the class. For each child, cut two acorns out of brown construction paper. Staple drawing paper inside the acorn shapes and trim to size. Have the children illustrate and write or dictate a story about a squirrel's adventures. You might help them by asking questions such as, "Where does the squirrel live?" "What are his or her friends like?" "What problems might the squirrel have?" "How does the squirrel solve his or her problems?"

★ Provide the children with brown, green, gray, and white paint. Ask the children to paint a picture of a squirrel gathering nuts in the fall.

★ Let the children make "Nutty Collages." Provide each child with a paper plate, yarn, glue, and different types of nuts or seeds. Have the children draw a simple squiggle shape on the plate with the glue. Show them how to lay the yarn on top of the glue and fill in the spaces with different types of nuts or seeds.

Movement Models

★ Play a game called "Who Stole My Nut?" Have the children sit in a semicircle. Choose one child to be the squirrel. This child sits in a chair with his or her back to the rest of the children. Place a brown paper nut under the chair. Have another child quietly come forward and take the nut. This child returns to his or her place in the circle and sits on the nut. The students then chant, "Squirrel, Squirrel, someone took your nut!" The squirrel tries to guess who has the nut. After three guesses, a new squirrel is chosen and the game continues.

★ Ask the children to pretend to be squirrels scampering through the trees and gathering nuts. If you wish, turn this into a game. Play music while the children scamper around. When the music stops, the children must freeze in position.

Squirrel Day #3

Feature Focus Read the book *Squirrel's Song*.

Learning Labs

★ Cut out squirrel and chipmunk shapes. On each squirrel write a lower-case letter. Write the corresponding capital letter on each chipmunk. Leave in a learning center. Have the children find the matching pairs of squirrels and chipmunks.

Think and Talk Time

★ Read the book to the children. Discuss the song that the chipmunk wrote for the squirrel. Have the class write additional verses about the squirrel using the same song format. Then ask the class to pretend they are squirrels and write a song about a chipmunk.

★ Have the class tell a group "add-on" story about a silly squirrel that brings home different objects instead of nuts. Start with the lines, "One day Silly Squirrel's mother sent him out to gather some nuts. But Silly Squirrel didn't bring home nuts, he brought _____." Have each child, in turn, suggest another line of the story. Repeat all previous story lines before you ask for the next line.

Project Pursuits

★ Have the children illustrate one of the versus they made up during *Think and Talk Time*. Give each child a precut circle, semicircles, and triangles and have them create a squirrel using the shapes. Help the children glue the shapes onto a piece of drawing paper. Provide some acorns and dried leaves for added texture. Ask the children to use crayons or markers to add in details and background. Display on a wall with the verses the children created.

★ Make "Nutty Squirrel Puppets." Provide each child with a precut squirrel shape and half a walnut shell. Let the children color the squirrel and glue the walnut to make the "body" as shown. After the glue has dried, ask the children to glue a tongue depressor to the back of the squirrel.

Movement Models

★ Make about twenty circles from brown construction paper. Call these circles acorns. Divide the class into two teams. Tell one group to cover their eyes while the other group hides the acorns. Explain that the acorns must be hidden so a little part of each acorn still shows. When all the acorns are hidden, tell the other group to find them. Count to see that all were found, then reverse the roles of the groups.

★ Play a game called "Find the Squirrel." Ask the children to pretend that they must find a silly gray squirrel that lives in a tree. Choose one child to be the squirrel. Have the rest of the children close their eyes while the squirrel hides somewhere in the play area. When you call out, "Let's Find the Squirrel!" the children open their eyes and search for the squirrel. When they find him or her, they must run back to a designated safe area. The squirrel tries to catch someone who will be the squirrel for the next game.

String Days

Pattern Page

String Days

Timing
   Spring
   During kite season
   During a music unit

What Children Bring
   A piece of string.

Previous Day Reminder
   A piece of ribbon tied around each child's finger.

Ready Resources

Books
   Bright, Robert. *Georgie and the Ball of Yarn.* New York: Doubleday, 1983.
   Calhoun, Mary. *The Battle of Reuben Robin and Kite Uncle John.* New York: Morrow, 1973. (See related activites, page 125.)
   Hillert, Margaret. *What Is It?* Cleveland, OH: Follett, 1978.
   Holland, Marion. *Big Ball of String.* New York: Random House, 1958. (See related activities, page 124.)
   Robinson, Nancy L. *The Missing Ball of String.* Easton, MD: Garrard, 1977.

Films
   ACI Media. *Stories in String.* Van Nuys, CA: AIMS Media, 1972.
   BBC. *String.* Paramus, NJ: Time-Life Film & Video, 1974.
   String Sounds. Los Angeles: Churchill Films, 1972. (See related activities, page 126.)

Records and Songs
   Penner, Fred. "I've Got No Strings." On *Special Delivery.* Shoreline Records. (SLN) 0027. (See related activities, page 124.)
   Glazer, Tom. "On Top of Spaghetti." In *Eye Winker, Tom Tinker, Chin Chopper.* New York: Doubleday, 1978.

Teacher Resources
   Capon, Jack. *Ball, Rope, and Hoop Activities.* Belmont, CA: David S. Lake, 1975.

String Day #1

Feature Focus Read the book *The Big Ball of String.* Listen to the song "I've Got No Strings."

Learning Labs

★ Let students pound nails randomly into wooden boards. Have them wrap different colors of yarn or string around the nails to make designs.

★ Place different lengths of yarn or string in a math area. Let the children measure the different pieces and sequence them by length.

Think and Talk Time

★ Have students share the pieces of string they brought from home. Ask each student to tell where the string came from and how it got to be the length it is. After all the children have shown their string, ask them to think of different ways in which to use their pieces of string. Record the children's answers.

★ Tie all the children's pieces of string together and measure the total length. Then show the children how to wind the string into a ball. Ask them why someone might want to save pieces of string in ball. Then read the book. Compare the size of the class string ball to the one in the book. How did the boy use his pieces of string? Compare the uses in the book to the list of children's responses.

Project Pursuits

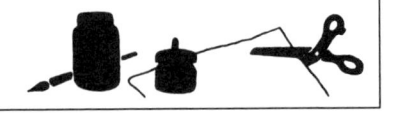

★ Have the children make "String Paintings." Have each child dip a piece of string into liquid tempera. Ask them to fold a piece of drawing paper in half and arrange the wet string on one side of the paper. Have the child fold the other side of the paper over the string, then hold the paper down gently and pull the string out. Unfold the papers and let dry. Display on a bulletin board under the caption "String Paintings."

★ Have the children make "String Sculptures." Give each child an inflated balloon. Have the child dip string into white glue and then wind the string around the balloon. String should be added until it covers most of the balloon's surface. Let dry. Then help the children pop the balloons and remove the fragments from inside the sculptures. Hang from light fixtures in the classroom.

Movement Models

★ Play "Cut the String." Have the children stand in a circle holding hands. They are the string. Choose one child to be the scissors. This child walks around the inside of the circle. At some point, the scissors "cuts the string," by tapping the hands of two adjacent players. These children must run around the circle, each in an opposite direction. Whoever returns to the empty spot in the circle first is the next scissors.

★ Give each child a yard of yarn or string. Ask the children to try different actions using the yarn or string. For example, you might ask them to make a box out of the string and then jump, hop, or crawl over and around it; lay the string in a line and jump back and forth over it; or make numbers or letters out of the string.

★ Let the children pretend to be puppets on strings. Then play the song and have the children pretend to be puppets without strings.

String Day #2

Feature Focus Read the book *The Battle of Rubin Robin and Kite Uncle John*.

Learning Labs

★ Make kites out of construction paper and write a different numeral on each. Attach the kites to a bulletin board with string hanging down from each as tails. Have the children put the correct number of clip clothespins on each kite's tail to match the numeral written on the kite.

★ Make twelve kite shapes out of paper. Attach a piece of string to each shape. Make sure that each piece of string is a different length (1"–12"). Place twelve library card pockets inside a file folder. Write a numeral, 1–12, on each. Have students measure the kites' tails, and put each kite in the correct pocket.

Think and Talk Time

★ Read the book to the children. How did the bird want to use the string? How did Uncle John want to use the string? Ask the children to pick words that describe the way the bird acted and the way Uncle John acted.

★ Brainstorm with the children to create a list of people or animals that use string. Have the children tell a story about one person and one animal who fight over a piece of string. How does each character want to use the string?

Project Pursuits

★ Let the children make "Bird's Nest Pencil Holders." Have each child paint a small can with white glue. Show the children how to wind the string tightly around the can—starting at the top and working down. Once the glue has dried, let the children paint their "nests."

★ Make "String Kites" with the class. Ask each child to glue or tie two sticks perpendicular to each other as shown. Supply the children with brightly colored pieces of yarn. Show them how to weave the yarn around the "X" of the two sticks. Start by tying a piece of yarn to one of the sticks. Pull the strand of yarn over the next crossbar, circle under the stick, and then back over the top. Pull the yarn to the next crossbar and do the same. Continue this process, always working in the same direction. Tie the end of the yarn to the stick when the design is finished.

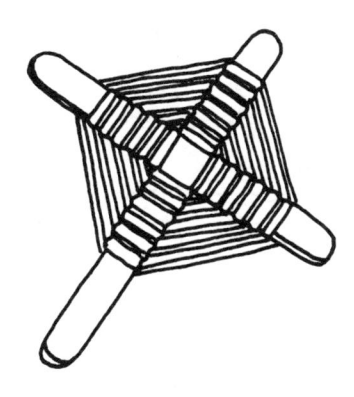

Movement Models

★ Provide each child with a piece of string. Ask them to pretend to be flying kites in the wind. Then ask them to pretend to be birds carrying the string home to make a nest.

★ Play "String Tag." Divide the class into two teams. Have each team stand on an opposite goal line, facing each other. Call one team the "Rubin Robins" and the other team "Kite Uncle Johns." Ask the Robins to turn their backs on the Uncle Johns. Then tell the Uncle Johns to quietly sneak up to the Robins. At some point call out "Uncle John is coming!" The Robins then chase the Uncle Johns back to their goal line. Any child who is tagged becomes part of the Robin team. Repeat, having the Robins sneak up to the Uncle Johns.

String Day #3

Feature Focus Watch the film *String Sounds*.

Learning Labs

★ Build a string instrument for the class to investigate. Place an eyescrew in each end of a 1" × 2" × 36" board. Tie nylon fishing line to each screw. Place a small plastic box or tub next to the instrument. Let the children pluck the string to hear the sound. Show them that pressing the box down on the string will change the sound that the string makes when plucked. Moving the box up and down the string will also change the sound.

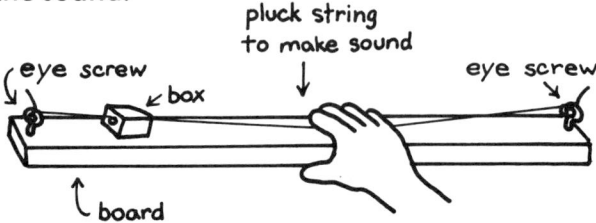

Think and Talk Time

★ Ask the children if they know what a stringed instrument is. Discuss different stringed instruments that the children may have seen or heard. Show the film after the discussion.

★ Invite a parent or person from the community to demonstrate a stringed instrument to the class. Encourage the person to explain how the various high and low sounds are created. If possible, have them play a short selection or two.

Project Pursuits

★ Play some orchestra music for the children. Then play the music again, and have the children draw a free design or picture. Ask them to use the colors that the music suggests to them. Have the children write or dictate a few sentences about what they thought of as they listened to the music. Display the pictures and writing on a classroom wall.

★ Have the children draw pictures of themselves playing stringed instruments. Encourage the children to add a background that shows where they are playing. Help the students title their pictures.

★ Let the children make "Cigar-Box Guitars." Provide each child with an empty, lidless cigar box or similar box. Also give each child four or five rubber bands of different thicknesses and lengths. Have the children place the rubber bands around the box. Show them how to pluck the bands to make different sounds. Point out the similarities between this instrument and other stringed instruments.

Movement Models

★ Ask the children to pretend to play different stringed instruments such as a guitar, a harp, a violin, and a cello. Play music as the children pantomime the movements.

★ Play a game called "My Harp!" Divide the class into groups of six or eight. Have each group sit in a circle. Choose a leader in each group. The leader (Child A) turns to the child on his or her right (Child B) and says, "Have you seen my harp?" Child B answers, "How does it play?" Child A replies, "Pluck, pluck, pluck," and pantomimes the motion of playing a harp. Then Child B turns to the child on his or her right, and starts the routine again. The children continue this question-response pattern until the original leader has had a chance to be Child B.

Teeny-Tiny Days

Pattern Page

128

Teeny-Tiny Days

Timing
   Anytime

What Children Bring
   Something teeny-tiny.

Previous Day Reminder
   A tiny (¼"-diameter) stick-on dot on each child's hand.

Ready Resources

Books
   Bridwell, Norman. *A Tiny Family.* New York: Scholastic, 1972. (See related activities, page 130.)
   DePaola, Tomie. *The Prince of the Dolomites.* San Diego, CA: Harcourt Brace Jovanovich, 1980.
   Galdone, Paul. *The Teeny Tiny Woman.* Boston: Houghton Mifflin, 1984.
   Hillert, Margaret. *Tom Thumb.* Cleveland, OH: Modern Curriculum Press, 1981. (See related activities, page 132.)
   Krasilovsky, Phyllis. *The Very Little Boy.* New York: Doubleday, 1962.
   Mosel, Arlene. *The Funny Little Woman.* New York: Dutton, 1972.
   Munsch, Robert, and Michael Martchenko. *The Boy in the Drawer.* Toronto, Canada: Annick Press, 1986. (See related activities, page 131.)

Films
   Teeny Tiny and the Witch Woman. Weston, CT: Weston Woods, 1980.

Records and Songs
   Raffi. "Thumbelina." On *Rise and Shine.* Shoreline Reocrds. (KSR) 8111.

Short Stories
   Andersen, Hans C. "Thumbelina." In *Han's Andersen's Fairy Tales.* L.K. Kingsland. New York: Oxford University Press, 1985. (See related activities, page 132.)
   Anderson, Paul S. "The Teeny Tiny Woman." In *Story Telling with the Flannel Board,* Book 1. Minneapolis, MN: Denison, 1963.
   Beskow, Elsa. "Tale of a Wee Little Woman." In *Read-To-Me Storybook.* Child Study Association of America. New York: Harper & Row, 1947.
   Brown, Margaret W. "Two Farmers." In *Read-To-Me Storybook.* Child Study Association of America. New York: Harper & Row, 1947.
   "One Inch Fellow." In *Favorite Fairy Tales Told in Japan.* Virginia Haviland. Boston: Little, Brown, 1967.

Teeny-Tiny Day #1

Feature Focus   Read the book *A Tiny Family*.

Learning Labs

★ Set up a teeny-tiny village for the children to play with. Draw streets and roads on the back of vinyl fabric. Supply small blocks for buildings and toy cars and trucks.

★ Let the children use tiny pieces of paper and tiny brushes to paint tiny pictures.

Think and Talk Time

★ Ask the children to tell you what makes something teeny-tiny. Discuss and list some other words that mean *tiny*. Ask the children to name some things that these words suggest to them.

★ Read the book. Discuss the way in which the tiny family uses regular-size objects. Brainstorm with the children to create a list of ways in which a tiny family could use some of the following: a soda-bottle top, a spool, a rubber band, a penny, a paper clip, and a pin. What could a tiny family use to make a bed? A house? A chair? A bathtub?

★ Have the children tell stories about what they would do if they discovered a tiny family living near their homes.

Project Pursuits

★ Divide the class into small groups. Let each group use materials from a junk or scrap box to make a room full of furniture, play equipment, or other items for tiny people. Encourage the children to use their imaginations. Display the items on Styrofoam meat trays.

★ Have the children make "Tiny People Puppets." Supply the children with small wooden ice-cream spoons, fine-tip felt pens, and scraps of paper or fabric. Ask the children to cut out and glue tiny clothes to the spoon. Show them how to draw faces on the puppets with the pens. Use an empty facial tissue box, which has the back cut out, for a puppet stage.

★ Have the children use tiny pieces of crayon to draw pictures of a tiny family they would like to meet. Encourage the children to include themselves in the picture.

Movement Models

★ Ask the children to think of different teeny-tiny animals, such as ants or spiders. Have the children pretend to be the tiny animals they think of. As they imitate the animals, call out movements such as forward, backward, to the left, to the right, fast, slow, and so on.

★ Play "Teeny-Tiny Toss" with the children. Give each child an empty egg carton. Ask the children to put the cartons on the floor and move a few steps back from them. Ask each child to toss a handful of buttons or other small objects, one piece at a time, into the egg carton. When all the students have finished, ask each child to count how many of the tiny objects landed in the egg carton sections.

Teeny-Tiny Day #2

Feature Focus Read the book *The Boy in the Drawer*.

Learning Labs

★ Obtain several small boxes. Cover the sides of each box with a different pattern of wallpaper or wrapping paper. Cut a small figure out of each piece of wallpaper or wrapping paper. Place the boxes and figures in a learning center. Have the children place each figure in the matching box.

★ Let the children make tiny people out of playdough.

Think and Talk Time

★ Discuss different places where tiny people could live. Encourage the children to suggest places in the classroom or on the playground. Ask the children to pretend a tiny little boy is looking for a home. Where might he live? You may want to have a doll handy so the children can visualize places where the "boy" could be.

★ Read the book. Compare the place where the boy lived to the places that the children suggested.

★ Ask the children what they would do if they woke up one morning and found out they had become as small as the boy in the book. Where would they live? Have the class tell stories about being tiny.

Project Pursuits

★ Have the children use fine-tip felt pens or crayons to draw a tiny picture of a place they would live if they were tiny. Ask the children to write or dictate a "teeny-tiny" bit of narrative to accompany their pictures. Display on a wall under the caption, "The Teeny-Tinys."

★ Give each child a tiny stick-on dot to incorporate into a picture about something tiny. Make a class book out of the pictures by placing the pictures inside a piece of folded construction paper. Have the class think of different titles for the book and vote on the best one. Write the title on the cover.

★ Have the children cut out pictures of tiny things from magazines or catalogs. Ask the children to make the pictures into a scene and glue the scenes on pieces of paper.

Movement Models

★ Play "The Boy in the Drawer." Choose one child to be the searcher. He or she should go out of the room. Pick another child to place a small doll somewhere in the room. The doll should not be covered in any way. Call the searcher back into the room and ask him or her to find the doll. The other children give clues to the child by clapping loudly when the child is moving closer to the doll and softly when the child is moving farther from the doll.

★ Play "Teeny-Tiny Tag." Ask the children to stand in a circle. Choose one child to go around the circle, tapping each child. The child should say "teeny-tiny," each time he or she taps someone. At some point, the child says, "tag!" The tagged child chases the first child around the circle and tries to tag the first child before he or she reaches the empty spot in the circle. If the child reaches the empty spot, the tagged child becomes the next tapper.

Teeny-Tiny Day #3

Feature Focus Read the book *Tom Thumb*.
Read the story "Thumbelina."

Learning Labs

★ Make "Thumb Cakes." Prepare a batch of cookie dough. Let the children use a thimble to cut out cookies. Bake carefully to avoid burning. Let the children eat the cookies for a snack. Serve with tiny glasses of milk. (Small glasses can be purchases at craft stores.)

★ Place small salad macaroni in an art area. Have the children string the macaroni on yarn or thread to make bracelets or necklaces. If you wish, color the macaroni pieces and encourage the children to develop repeating patterns.

Think and Talk Time

★ Obtain doll house objects, such as chairs, lamps, rugs, and tables. Have the children compare the size of the objects to regular-size objects in the classroom. Then ask the children to compare the size of their thumbs to the size of their bodies. What would it be like to be a person the size of a thumb? Read the book and the story to the children. Discuss the advantages and disadvantages of being so small.

Project Pursuits

★ Let the children make "Thumbprint People." Have each child make a thumbprint on a piece of paper. Then have the children use fine-tip felt pens and scraps of paper to turn the thumbprint into a person. Ask the children to write or dictate a story about the teeny-tiny person. Display under the caption "You're No Bigger Than My Thumb."

★ Let the children make teeny-tiny books about adventures they would have if they were as small as a thumb. Give each child a 6" × 3" piece of paper. Have the children fold the papers in half. Ask them to pretend they are very small and to draw pictures that show where they live and an adventure they might have. Add more pages if needed. Place the final books inside another piece of folded construction paper. Let students title their own books.

Movement Models

★ Play a game called "Teeny, Tiny." Choose one player to be IT. IT stands on a goal line. The other children stand about 30 feet away in a row opposite to the IT. Facing the group, IT calls, "Teeny," and the row of children take very tiny steps toward the goal line. At irregular intervals, IT calls out, "Tiny," and turns his or her back to the group. The children then take heel-to-toe steps. The game continues until one of the children reaches the goal line. This child becomes the next IT.

★ Play a game called "Tom Thumb." Mark off two goal lines some distance apart. Choose one child to be IT. This child stands between the goal lines and calls out, "Tom Thumb!" three times. On the third call, the rest of the class runs from one goal line to the other. IT tries to tag the children as they run. Tagged students help IT catch other students.

Umbrella Days

Pattern Page

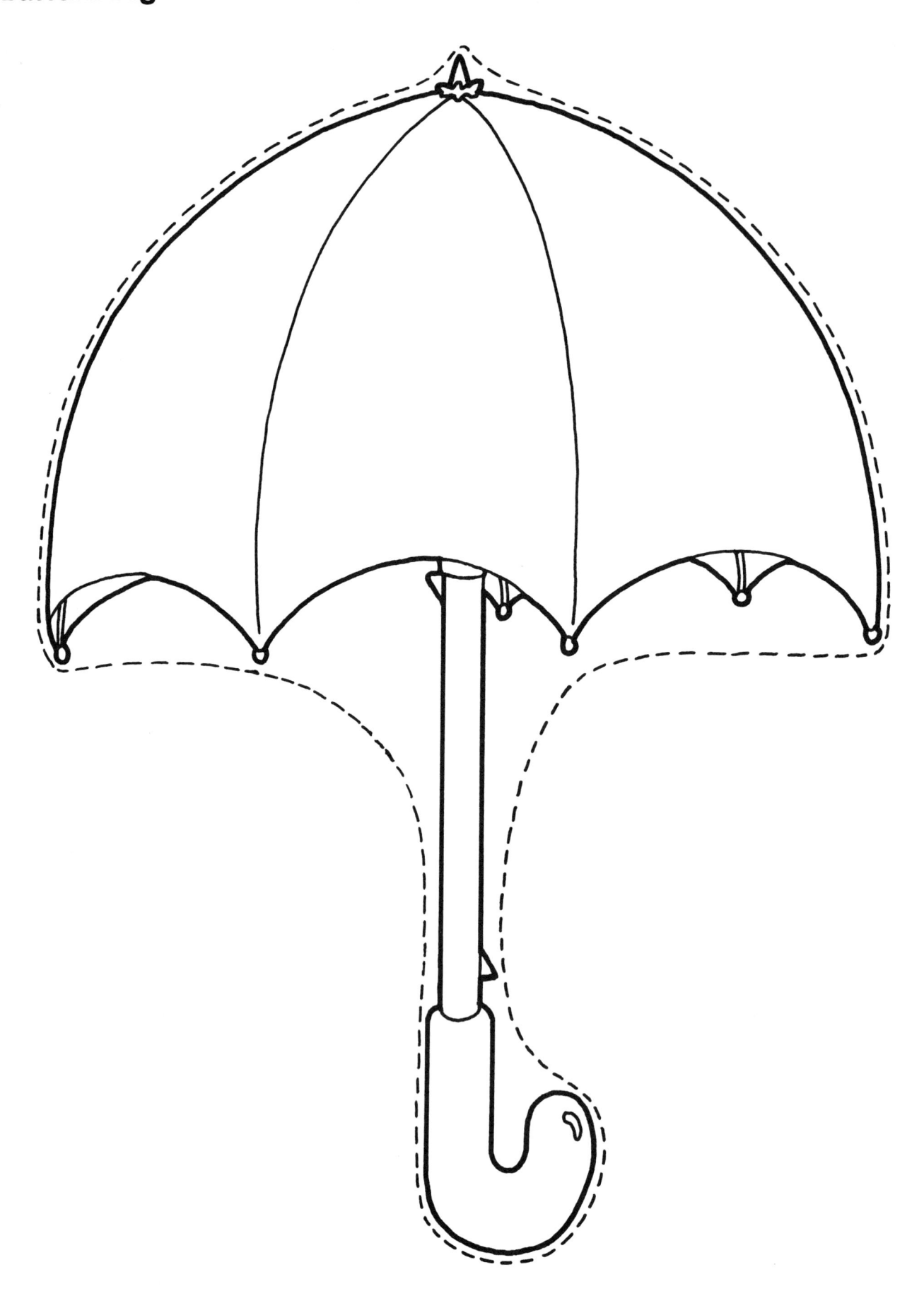

Umbrella Days

Timing
   During the rainy season

What Children Bring
   An umbrella.

Previous Day Reminder
   A construction-paper umbrella pinned to each child's shirt.

Ready Resources

Books
   Blance, Ellen, et al. *Monster and the Magic Umbrella*. Los Angeles: Bowmar-Noble.
   Bright, Robert. *My Red Umbrella*. New York: Morrow, 1959. (See related activities, page 137.)
   Ginsburg, Mirra. *Mushroom in the Rain*. New York: Macmillan, 1978. (See related activities, page 137.)
   LaRue, Mabel G. *Tiny's Big Umbrella*. Boston: Houghton Mifflin, 1964.
   Pinkwater, Daniel. *Roger's Umbrella*. New York: Dutton, 1982. (See related activities, page 138.)
   Tobias, Tobi. *Umbrella Named Umbrella*. New York: Knopf, 1976.
   Yashima, Taro. *Umbrella*. New York: Viking-Penguin, 1977. (See related activities, page 136.)

Films
   Kratky Films, Czechoslovakia. *Mole and the Umbrella*. Del Mar, CA: CRM/McGraw-Hill Films, 1973.

Poems
   Esbensen, Barbara J. "Umbrellas." In *Read-Aloud Rhymes for the Very Young*. Jack Prelutsky, ed. New York: Knopf, 1986.
   Merriam, Eve. "Bella Had a New Umbrella." In *Blackberry Ink*. New York: Morrow, 1985.
   Scott, Louise B. "Umbrellas in My Colors." In *Rhymes for Learning Times*. Minneapolis, MN: Denison, 1984.

Records and Songs
   "I Love It When It Rains." On *Love*. Birdwing Records. (BDW) KB-43005.
   Sesame Street. *Let a Frown Be Your Umbrella*. Sesame Street Records. (SSR) 22061.

Short Stories
   Anderson, Paul S. "The First Umbrella." In *Story Telling with the Flannel Board*, Book 2. Minneapolis, MN: Denison, 1970. (See related activities, page 136.)
   Lenski, Lois. "The Duck Umbrella." In *Read-To-Me Storybook*. Child Study Association of America. New York: Harper & Row, 1947.

Umbrella Day #1

Feature Focus   Read the story "The First Umbrella" and the book *Umbrella*.

Learning Labs

★ Make edible umbrellas for snacks. Toast pieces of bread and let each child use a cookie cutter to cut a circle out of the toast. Cut a small hole in each circle. Let the children spread the circles with cream cheese or peanut butter. Give each child a carrot stick to stick through the hole in the circle. Let the children hold up their "umbrellas" as they eat them.

★ Cut out umbrella shapes from construction paper. Write a numeral on each one. Also cut out raindrop shapes. Place the umbrellas and the raindrops in a math center. Have the children place the correct raindrop on each umbrella.

Think and Talk Time

★ Have the children sit under the umbrellas they brought from home as you read the story and the book. How were umbrellas really invented? Discuss possible answers with the children.

★ Brainstorm with the children to create a list of possible ways in which to use an umbrella, besides the obvious answer of keeping dry. Use the list of ideas to create stories about a little girl who gets an umbrella when it isn't raining.

Project Pursuits

★ Have students make "Egg-Carton Umbrellas." Give each child a single egg-carton section. Let the children cut the sections in half and glue the open sides to pieces of paper. Show them how to add pipe-cleaner handles to make umbrellas. Ask them to add details and backgrounds to their pictures.

★ Ask the students to draw a picture that illustrates an unusual use for an umbrella. Give each child a precut umbrella shape to incorporate into the picture. Encourage the children to show the person or animal who is using the umbrella. Ask each child to write or dictate narration about his or her picture. Display on a classroom wall or bulletin board.

Movement Models

★ Ask the children to pretend they are walking in a rainstorm. Let them creatively move and talk about what they are doing. Ask the children to use pretend umbrellas in their movements.

★ Place several open umbrellas on the floor so the undersides of the umbrellas are facing up. Supply the children with rolled-up pairs of socks or yarn balls. Have the children try to throw the socks or balls into the open umbrellas. Ask them to count the number of times they get a sock or ball inside.

★ Have an "Umbrella Relay." Divide the class into teams. Place a closed umbrella for each team some distance away from the children. Tell the children that each child has to run to the umbrella, open it, turn around three times, close it, and run back to tag the next person in line. Emphasize umbrella safety before starting the race.

Umbrella Day #2

Feature Focus Read the book *My Red Umbrella* or *Mushroom in the Rain*.

Learning Labs

★ Cut out different sizes of umbrellas from construction paper. Leave in a learning area. Have the children sequence the umbrellas by size—smallest to largest.

★ Leave bright colors of paint in an art area. Have children paint umbrellas.

Think and Talk Time

★ Have the children share the umbrellas they brought from home. Ask the children to open the umbrellas and to sort them by size or by color.

★ Ask the children if they have ever had to share an umbrella with someone. What was it like? Could both people fit under the umbrella? Let the children share stories about trying to stay dry under an umbrella.

★ Read one of the books to the children. How many people or animals were under the umbrella or mushroom? Look closely at the pictures—were all the creatures dry? Ask the children to describe what it would be like to have a magic umbrella that got larger when they needed it to.

Project Pursuits

★ Let the children make "Umbrella Dioramas." Have them use miniature umbrellas (available from novelty or craft stores), pipe cleaner or paper figures, and a shoe box to illustrate one of the scenes in the book. Have the children write or dictate a few remarks about his or her scene. Display in the classroom.

★ Make a "movie" to retell one of the stories. Have each child illustrate one of the scenes in the book. When the pictures are finished, tape them all together and roll them onto a paper towel tube. Attach the tube to a box. Retell the story as you unwind the pictures from the tube.

★ Make a large class umbrella. Lay a large piece of butcher paper on the floor. Outline an umbrella shape on the paper. Let each child decorate a small section of the umbrella with paper, paints, or crayons. Display on a wall.

Movement Models

★ Use a parachute to create a large umbrella. Lay the parachute on the floor and have the children stand around it. Show them how to hold onto the parachute with an overhand grasp. Once the children have lifted the parachute, call out movements for them to follow. For example, you might ask two children to run under the umbrella and switch places, you could have the children move the "umbrella" up and down, or you could have the class move in different directions as they hold on to the "umbrella." At the end of the period, ask all the children to crawl under the parachute and let it fall on them.

★ Have students pantomime the story as you read to them. You might want to divide the class into small groups so each child can play the role of one creature.

Umbrella Day #3

Feature Focus Read the book *Roger's Umbrella*.

Learning Labs

★ Put several umbrellas in the creative dress-up area to encourage role-playing.

★ Cut several umbrellas out of different patterns and textures of wallpaper or fabric. Cut out raincoats to match the umbrellas. Leave in a learning center. Have children match the umbrellas to the raincoats.

Think and Talk Time

★ Ask the children to describe what it would be like to own a magic umbrella. What would the umbrella do? Where could it take you? What would it look like? Have the children consider what would happen if the umbrella did things by itself.

★ Read the book to the children. How did Roger learn to control his umbrella? Ask the children what they think each command word meant. What would they say to their umbrellas to make them go up or down? Fast or slow?

Project Pursuits

★ Have the children use their imaginations to create "Magic Umbrellas." Provide each child with an umbrella outline. Have the children use a variety of materials such as paper, glue, sewing trims, pipe cleaners, Q-tips, buttons, sequins, and yarn to decorate the umbrellas. Ask the children to dictate or write a few sentences that describe what the umbrellas can do. Display under the caption, "Our Magic Umbrellas."

★ Have the children create a classroom book titled, "The Adventures of the Magic Umbrellas." Ask each child to contribute a drawing that shows him or her doing something with a magic umbrella. Make sure they show an umbrella and a background in the pictures. Have each child dictate or write about his or her adventures with the umbrella. Place the pages inside a piece of folded construction paper. Write the title on the cover.

Movement Models

★ Have each child carry the umbrella that he or she brought from home. Pretend you are Roger and give the "umbrellas" directions to follow. Have the children do various movements with the umbrellas.

★ Play the "Umbrella Game." Choose two children to be the "umbrellas." These children hold hands and raise their arms up high to form the umbrella. The other children stand in a single-file line and march under the umbrella in time to music. When the music stops, the child under the umbrella stands to the side. When a second child is caught, the two trapped children form the next umbrella.

★ Let each child open his or her umbrella and stand apart from the rest of the children. Play music and ask the children to dance in time to the music with their umbrellas.